Listening to the Sound of His Voice

from Childhood
...to Grandparenthood

by
Nan McKenzie Kosowan

Listening to the Sound of His Voice - From Childhood to Grandparenthood

© 2008 Nan McKenzie Kosowan

All rights reserved.

International Standard Book Number: 978-1-896213-42-2

Published in Canada by:
byDesign Media
12730 Simcoe Street, Port Perry L9L 1B3
E-mail diane@bydesignmedia.ca
www.bydesignmedia.ca
Layout and Design: Diane Roblin-Lee

Names used in this book are not always the actual names of the people in these true stories.

Unless otherwise noted, all Scriptural references are transcribed from The New King James Version of the Bible, Thomas Nelson Publishers © 1984, 1982, 1980, 1979.

Library and Archives Canada Cataloguing in Publication

Kosowan, Nan McKenzie, 1928-
     Listening to the sound of His voice : from childhood-- to grandparenthood / Nan McKenzie Kosowan.

Includes index.
ISBN 978-1-896213-42-2

     1. Spiritual life--Christianity. 2. Listening--Religious aspects--Christianity. 3. God (Christianity)--Knowableness. 4. Holy Spirit. I. Title.

BV4501.3.K68 2008   C2008-903556-9

—✑ Dedication ✑—

This book is dedicated to believers who want to hear from God in everyday events, whether of joy or crisis.

Those who have that communication, have a rich relationship with the Lord that provides daily comfort, caution, encouragement, warning, strength and wisdom to equip them for every relationship, every instance of their lives as they choose to listen and to obey what they hear.

Those who would like to have such communication with the Lord may not realize it is possible. If they have not tried, they may think Creator God has more important matters to concern Himself over than their life events. Those who have tried, because they have chosen to listen, will encourage others that God delights to communicate with us, whom He has created in His own image.

There is nothing like the story of a real person's intimate relationship with God to encourage others to try it for themselves. Whether seeker, believer or skeptic, reading these true stories may show you how you too can communicate with God as you call on His Holy Spirit and listen for His reply in whatever way He chooses to give it to you.

What guarantee do we have that we are hearing from the Lord? The Bible tells us in John 1:1-4, John 17:5, 1 John 5:11 and 1 John 5: 20 that Jesus Christ was the Word made flesh. If we believe in Jesus, we can believe that Scripture, which is God's own Word, will confirm any word we may believe we have received from Him.

Can we hear from God?

…if we choose to listen!

My sheep hear My voice, and I know them, and they will follow Me (John 10:27).

Can we hear from God? If we do choose to listen, how do we recognize that it is God communicating with us?

Listening for His love, comfort, patience and strength, we may find His thoughts among our thoughts, in the remembrance of a scripture verse, in a response springing up in our hearts or in a conversation we have with someone. We may receive His answer to a pressing problem through something we read, an unexpected incident, even a quickened memory from the past that supplies pertinent information we need.

Whatever way God uses to reach us by His Spirit, it will always ring with the truth found in His written Word.

As we seek His input, it is as though we have our ears tuned to listen for His voice in whatever way He wants to make it heard.

When we do receive His guidance, how do we share it? We interpret our experience for others in ways we normally express ourselves. Some of the most celebrated expressions of God speaking into real people's lives are found in the psalms of the Bible.

As we listen and follow the leading of God's Holy Spirit, we become equipped and empowered in Jesus' way of handling life's joys and challenges. Staying alert and tuned in to hear from Him becomes both a privilege and a necessity.

We start our adventure of hearing God's voice with the story of a skeptic who, like many people today including Christians, did not realize that the Creator of the universe deeply desires to speak into each of our lives, whether we are experiencing a small trial or a major, unexpected crisis. When he heard how God's Holy Spirit had brought victory out of someone's desperate situation, he was encouraged to try listening for what God might have to say about his own problem.

The stranger wanted to talk. He had dropped into our after-church coffee time and joined a little group of us standing by the coffee machine. He made a brief comment that invited response. Though I can't remember his comment, I well remember his reaction to my response.

"When I was in a difficult situation something like that," I began, "I asked the Lord what He ...."

The stranger broke in somewhat incredulously, "I hope you didn't expect an answer." He was serious.

"Oh, but I did," I said, realizing I was talking about an experience unfamiliar to him. "Indeed, I get quite cross with myself when I'm faced with a problem and forget to ask for the help God always has for me."

"You really mean that, don't you?" he asked, looking curious, probably thinking that I was going to tell him about some voice crashing through the clouds or piping through the kitchen tap.

I laughed at my own thought (I sometimes think in cartoons) and shared with him the happy outcome of my situation when I used the wisdom the Lord gave me as He had dropped His thoughts in among my own thoughts.

The visitor's face relaxed and he began to share another situation that had been troubling him, wondering "if God would have something to say about it."

Standing there at the coffee machine, we shared with him the scriptural response that would help with his situation. God was using our little group around the coffee machine to speak to our guest.

The highlight of the morning for all of us was our visitor's openness to hear about God's concern for him, his every problem, every good happening, every hope and every plan he had.

It was Alice, the youngest member among us who asked our visitor the most important question. "We're talking about the Lord, but it must be hard for you to understand what we're saying if you don't know Who He is. Would you like to meet Jesus? We can pray with you if you'd like us to."

He nodded cautiously and we prayed together with him, knowing this first step would open up a new world for him.

Our visitor became a faithful, enthusiastic member of our church. He particularly treasured the opportunity to share with visitors what the Lord was doing in his life as long as he would remember to look into God's Word and listen for His voice. He discovered that answers from the Lord always bless, are always biblical and always carry the marks of God's loving, wise character.

All through the Bible, we read how God spoke to people. He continues to speak into lives today. *Listening to the Sound of His Voice...* shares adventures in asking for and receiving from God help needed for life situations as a child, friend, spouse, parent, grandparent and a caregiver of an aging parent. It also draws on over forty years' experience serving on church lay teams, praying and counseling with people who were earnestly seeking answers from God.

That the final and longest chapter is "Listening...as a work in progress," testifies to the fact that relationship with the Lord is an ever-growing, never-ending wonder to be delighted in, practiced and shared.

As you read through the true stories of this book, perhaps you will recall times when God's Holy Spirit has led you in similar ways. May you be encouraged to keep listening for the sound of His voice.

Names used in this book are not always the actual names of the people in these true stories.

Eye has not seen, nor ear heard, nor have entered into the heart of man the things which God has prepared for those who love Him. But God has revealed them to us through His Spirit. For the Spirit searches all things, yes, the deep things of God (1 Corinthians 2: 9, 10).

The spirit of a man is the lamp of the Lord, searching all the inner depths of his heart (Proverbs 20: 27).

The entrance of Your words gives light (Psalm 119: 130).

How sweet are Your words to my taste. Sweeter than honey to my mouth! (Psalm 119: 103).

How precious are Your thoughts to me, O God! How great is the sum of them! If I should count them, they would be more in number than the sand. When I awake, I am still with You (Psalm 139: 17,18).

—᠗ Contents ᠗—

3: LISTENING...AS A SPOUSE

4: LISTENING...AS A PARENT

5: LISTENING... AS A GRANDPARENT

6: LISTENING...AS A CAREGIVER OF AN AGING PARENT

7: LISTENING...
AS A WORK IN PROGRESS

BIOGRAPHY

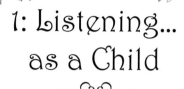

1: Listening...
as a Child

"Mommy, God Just Talked To Me."

Can a child hear from God?

I climbed the stairs from my basement playroom to find Mother in the kitchen. With all the solemnity a seven-year-old could muster I said, "Mommy, God just talked to me."

In our home, we said grace at mealtimes but we weren't a church-going family. Mother straightened up, cleared her throat and said very quietly, "Oh, and what did He say?"

"When I was putting Kitty in his basket for his nap and the sun was coming through the window on me, God said He loved me. Mommy, it felt so good."

Mother brushed off her apron and said, "Well, why don't you go back downstairs and play." She never spoke of that incident again.

But for me, at seven years of age, that simple, unexpected moment created an expectancy of God that I have never lost. Today, the memory of it reminds me that God can do whatever He wants, whenever He wants.

Samuel's Experience

When I became a Christian 20 years later, I thought of that moment in my basement playroom when I was a child as I read 1 Samuel 3:4. The story is of Samuel as a boy, serving the aging prophet Eli. It says clearly that Samuel had never heard God's voice and indeed did not yet know the Lord.

This intriguing story starts in chapter three: "...and while Samuel was lying down...the Lord called Samuel. And he answered, 'Here I am.'

"So he ran to Eli and said, 'Here I am, for you called me.' And he said, 'I did not call; lie down again.' And he went and lay down...

"...Now Samuel did not yet know the Lord, nor was the word of the Lord yet revealed to him.

"And the Lord called Samuel again. So he arose and went to Eli and said, 'Here I am for you did call me.' Then Eli perceived the Lord had called the boy.

"Therefore Eli said to Samuel, 'Go, lie down and it shall be if He calls you, that you must say, 'Speak, Lord for your servant hears.' So Samuel went and lay down in his place.

"Now the Lord came and stood and called as at the other times, 'Samuel! Samuel!' And Samuel answered, "Speak for your servant hears."

Anytime, Anywhere to Anyone

Again, some years later, I recalled both that Bible story about little Samuel and the Lord's sweet message to me as a small girl as I listened to the Christian television program, 100 Huntley Street. A Muslim woman was telling her story of searching in prayer for answers to perplexing personal problems.

When she heard comfort and assurances from a voice she had never heard before, she asked, "Who is that speaking?"

The answer came, "It is the Spirit of Jesus, the Son of God, who speaks to you."

The next morning, the woman made her way to a house nearby where she'd heard a Christian missionary woman was living.

She knocked at the door to ask, "I understand you know this Jesus. How can I come to know Him too?"

God is God. If He wants to speak into a life before someone has met His Son Jesus, He can do that. How often does He speak with love, comfort, wisdom, direction and warning into the lives of people who don't, at that time, recognize it as His voice?

Who better to tell them whose voice it is than believers who've learned to listen for the sound of His voice?

ꓗ Sermon From a Six-Year-Old

can start a mom thinking!

If sermons are supposed to get us thinking, my six-year-old was preaching to his mom on that morning 47 years ago.

"Mommy", said my little guy, looking earnest and puzzled, "You are always busy doing something. And Daddy is too. But you do the same stuff again the next day and then the day after that and all the other days too. Daddy's busy, but he does something and it's done and he doesn't have to do it again for a long time."

It was one of those "Huh?" times. Something was going on in his little head and I wasn't getting it. I thought I'd better employ a little motherly diplomacy at this point.

"Like what, dear? What is it Mommy's doing that she has to do again and again?"

"Well, there's cleaning and meals and making beds and doing laundry" he said, ticking off his fingers.

"And Daddy's things that he doesn't have to keep doing all the time?" I prompted, thinking maybe he was wondering if moms have to work in circles because they didn't do things right the first time. Maybe he thought dads must do things right because they didn't have to keep repeating everything they do?

"Daddy's things?" said Larry. "Well, he paints the house and that's that. He cuts the grass and that's good till later when it gets long. He musta put those big stones down the side of the house right cuz he doesn't have to bother with them anymore. Why do you do things over all the time?"

I wanted to laugh but this looked like a matter he'd been doing some serious thinking about. I thought I should treat it seriously too. Perhaps it was an opportunity to help him with something that was bothering him, though I wasn't sure what that was. I was sure God knew what was going on in that little mind. I just had to hear from the Lord so I could help.

"Well," I started carefully, "to start with, I do things that have to be done every day. You have to eat three times a day…"

"…maybe even four or five times a day," he grinned, his eyebrows flying high, "and you get me my apple and cookie outa the fridge, every day after school, don'tcha?"

"And Daddy goes to work every day, day after day," I said.

"And he comes home for supper every night," he put in, his eyebrows going up again in the process of discovery.

"You're getting it, aren't you," I smiled as I got his apple and cookie out of the fridge.

"Yah," he said, "I can see. You do things lots because we need them lots. Daddy does things we don't need so much."

Well, I thought, I don't think we'll tell Daddy that in just that way! But I did say, "There are things both Daddy and I decide to do and will keep doing because they're needed all the time by those we love and we want to help them be happy and healthy. Then there are other things we decide to do that are one-time things, things that keep going after we start them and we just need to check every once in a while to see if they're doing what they're supposed to be doing."

"Like Daddy taking the car somewhere to get fixed when it sounds funny every once in a while," he said thoughtfully, "because we need the car to shop and go to church."

"You have got it!" I laughed, pumping his hand up and down. "If you think something is important, you decide to keep on doing it, whether it needs to be done every day or just once in a while. The thing is, you have to think about it, ask God about it to see if it's important and think how you could do it well. Then you make up your mind to keep doing it or to keep checking it out as long as it's needed. You want to do that because it's going to help someone else if you do."

"Well, I promise to put my pajamas away in the morning, Mommy," he said as he set aside this junior philosophy class to run outside to his swing.

Is he catching on to the meaning of being responsible for his actions? I smiled to myself as my little guy stopped and came back to close the door behind him.

Does that sound like a sermon to keep tucked under one's belt? The Lord must be pleased to touch little ones in ways that will affect them all their lives as they watch the loving actions of family around them to bless others.

I remember thinking those many years ago that the word, "responsible" wouldn't be big in our son's vocabulary yet. But if he was getting the idea at six that bode well for his future life involvements, including decisions taken and kept for the sake of loved ones who will need him and his loyalty in the years ahead when I get to be a grandma.

Prayers Of A Child Touch Heaven

to bring victory over drowning, a broken home and cancer

Holly comes from a family that believes that "God's Word is true, that He hears our prayers and rejoices when we practise what we believe, not waiting for doubts to creep in."

Holly was just eight when the Lord answered her prayer to save her baby sister's life.

Holding to the wall, at the deep end of the neighbor's pool where the family was spending the afternoon, Holly was practising her kick when she saw three-year-old Lara lean over the pool's edge and fall in. She watched in horror as the little orange bathing suit plummeted towards the bottom. Holly cried out in her heart, "Oh God, please help me save Lara!"

With eyes fastened on the disappearing orange suit, Holly threw herself after her sister and somehow caught the strap of her suit and pulled her to the surface. Within seconds she had Lara sitting back from the pool's edge.

"Mommy," said Holly, her eyes wide with amazement and joy, "God had me here to save Lara when she fell in. I asked

Him quick to help me and He said to keep my eye on her orange suit. I did and I got her back in a wink."

Mother Judy who had turned for just that wink of a minute to speak to her neighbor, now gathered her two girls in her arms and thanked the Lord passionately. "They're never too young to learn to lean on the Lord," she told her impressed neighbor.

Judy loves to share one of her family's favorite scriptures:

> *Be kindly affectionate to one another with brotherly love, in honor giving preference to one another; not lagging in diligence, fervent in spirit, serving the Lord; rejoicing in hope, patient in tribulation, continuing steadfastly in prayer, distributing to the needs of the saints, given to hospitality* (Romans 12: 10-12).

Brandon had cancer when he was very young. He accepted the chemotherapy with the pragmatism of a three-year-old, never questioning the high hospital operating table, the needles or the injections until one day he came under an attack of such fear that hospital attendants had to hold him down to administer his weekly dosage. That continued for six weeks.

His grandmother fasted and prayed, his family prayed and his dad brought home an animated video that told the story, from Mark 4: 37-40, of Jesus and His disciples in a great storm that threatened to engulf their boat. Fascinated, Brandon watched Jesus rebuke the windstorm and the disciples who had been shaking with fear just minutes before, pick up their oars and row confidently home.

That day, Brandon got the Lord's message in his three-year-old heart: in threatening situations, Jesus' presence calms fear. He was ready to face his "fear storm" with confidence that Jesus would bring His calm every time Brandon went for treatment.

The next day he went skipping down the hospital hall to therapy, hugging staff people he knew on his way. Once on the treatment table he sang at the top of his voice, "Here we are together, together, together. Here we are together, just praising the Lord," much to the delight of hospital staff who just the week before had held his quaking little body down for the usual needle.

After another year of treatment, Brandon was declared free of cancer.

Today, he approaches his teens without a vestige of the disease. This young man of faith and twinkling eyes knows Jesus heals. He jumps at the opportunity to share that truth if telling his story can help someone who needs to hear it.

When Brandon and younger brother Justin were not yet in their teens, they knew they were far from being marriage counselors, but they knew where to turn when they saw a household crumbling.

There was only one thing to do when they saw their school chum Allan's horrified face and heard the painful news that his parents were leaving each other. They joined hands, closed their eyes and called on the Lord to bring Allan's parents together again. For a year and a half they continued to pray that way, listening to the Lord's assurances that all would be well and that they should continually remind Allan that God hears and answers prayers.

When Allan's parents came back together and his home was once again restored, Allan and his two prayer warrior chums "hung out" together at every opportunity. His parents' appreciation for the support given their son was evident as they gave full permission for his visits to Brandon and Justin's home.

"They're 'pre-Christians,' at the moment," says Brandon as he and Justin share a big smile, "but that will change, because now they've seen God's heart for them."

—❧❧—

Getting Lost, Getting Home

a boy's prayer saves a man

Joyce was full of that special kind of excitement that seems to underline her passion for stories with a neat ending, especially if it's about a troubled life making a successful u-turn back to the Lord

"Peter's funeral was one of the best I've ever attended," she said brightly, clapping her hands together as though to catch and hold the memory. "It was as much about a reclaimed life as about the death of our dear, wonderful friend Peter."

Of all the memories shared by family and friends at the service, one by the dead man's brother John, particularly moved her. She knew that John had lived on the "wild side" of life. She'd been praying that his big brother Peter's peace, Christian living and the testimony of friends who spoke at the funeral would touch John. But it was John's testimony that affected them all.

When John spoke, he told of a bittersweet childhood experience in his homeland of Holland, during the Second World War. Every week, he and his big brother would pull their sleds over the fields and the frozen canal to get wood for cooking and heat. They always looked forward to going because the neighbor always gave them supper before they left for home.

On one of those trips, when John was nine years old, he and his big brother got lost. They were cold and crying, trying to get home through sudden, heavy fog. They trudged endlessly in circles until Peter said they should stop, fold their hands, bow their heads and pray for God's help to find their way home.

After they prayed, the boys wandered for some time, still not knowing where they were going, until John burst out in exasperation and fear, "It doesn't work! Prayer doesn't work!"

His big brother stopped and said, "Well, we'll pray again. God answers prayer." The two children prayed once more. At that moment, the sun broke through the fog. They saw where they were and headed gratefully for home.

"Sometimes we get lost in life, really lost," John told the mourners, most of whom knew that as a grown man John had strayed from the Lord for many years.

"But two years ago, God spoke to my heart," he said, "reminding me of that time in Holland during the war when we were lost as kids. I stopped, folded my hands, bowed my head and prayed for God's help to find my way home. I was praying the same prayer again. And God has answered my prayer again."

Joyce was quiet for a moment after recounting John's story. "You know, that adventure in the fog when he was a little kid is more than just a cute tale," she said. "John's brother had given him the keys to safe return and prayer got him back home to his loved ones not once, but twice! We can all hope someone will boast over us at our funerals someday like John boasted over his big brother Peter."

Point your kids in the right direction. When they're old, they won't be lost (Proverbs 22:6 - The Message Version).

A Gift Of Music

a son steps out to bless with a creative idea from God

As usual, the young man ushered me ahead of him onto the church platform. As usual, he took his place in front of the microphone to play the opening bars of the music we were presenting.

But that Good Friday morning, the young man did not strum a guitar introduction as usual. Instead, he leaned down behind the lectern and drew out his oboe, cached away there before the service for just this moment.

My surprise turned to immediate identification with the oboe's plaintive strains intoning, "Man of sorrows, acquainted with grief."

The musical introduction completed, he picked up his guitar and nodded me in. With his accompaniment I sang that moving piece of music in a way I'd never sung it before.

"The Lord told me it would help set the mood," he grinned after the service, "so I practised the intro with the oboe instead of the guitar."

With a twinkle in his eye, he added, "The surprise was my own idea...I think."

I was always delighted to have the young man, my son, accompany me musically. But that day he gave me a precious present as I witnessed his connection with our God who gives us gifts to reveal His presence among us.

Let us consider how to stir up one another to love and good works (Hebrews 10:24 RSV).

2: Listening...
as a Friend

Tea And Sympathy...
Or Tea And Sensitivity

when you want to hear the truth

I dropped the expected package off at my new neighbor's door. Coreen took one look at my face which had misery written all over it and drew me in for a cup of tea. I sank down into my neighbor's overstuffed sofa, embarrassed that my struggle with my problem was so obvious. But her concern and the comforting of her sofa eased my tension a bit as we waited for the kettle to boil.

I can still see her big, solicitous eyes searching my face for indications of how deep my hurt ran as she handed me my cup of tea. She was a good listener and asked all the best questions to loosen me up. I hadn't meant to tell her my troubles, but it felt so good to have someone care that I spilled it all right into her lap.

She meant well, but the next half hour with Coreen proved the most unrewarding time of sharing I had spent since becoming a new Christian the year before. In that time, I had come to appreciate believing sisters and brothers who would listen to a problem and then share comments from the Word of God, not from mere opinion.

My new neighbor did not realize that when Christians share their problems together, they are looking to the Word of God for answers as the Holy Spirit helps them apply that Word to their problem. But she knew an aching heart when she saw it and gave what she had: tea and sympathy.

I appreciated her caring, but noticed as I got up to leave that my thoughts were turned even more inward than when I'd arrived. With good intention she had drawn me in for tea...and, unintentionally, into a pity party.

I knew I had to get to Betty's.

Betty was my spiritual big sister and was always ready to hear my problems as a young Christian if I'd become too caught up in myself to ask for the Lord's advice. This time was no different.

There was also an overstuffed sofa at Betty's and I sank into it as soon as I arrived. But this time it was tea and sensitivity I received - Betty's sensitivity to hear what the Holy Spirit had to say. After I dumped my problem, Betty cocked her head, smiled, grabbed my hands between her own and said, "Okay, let's pray. But we have to pray God's Word back to Him. It's His Word He agrees with, you know. If it's His Word we're praying, He'll see that it happens."

But even as I wept for the rebellious part I'd played in the problem we were praying about, I thought about my new neighbor. One day it might be her hands I'd be holding in prayer to address a problem she might have. I was learning the Word of God and I prayed that the Holy Spirit would minister to her in my company as wonderfully as He was ministering to me now through Betty's kind but uncompromising advice from Scripture.

A Life Rooted In Jesus

...is more than a copycat Christianity

An inner-city church worker with great social enthusiasm came to our young suburban church to gather recruits for a year of service. The volunteers would befriend members of his community who had little, either materially or spiritually.

His address stirred my social conscience as it hadn't been stirred since university days when, as a reporter on the student newspaper, I'd thrown myself into debate over social issues of the day.

"The aim of this program," the young man told our congregation, "is to see Christian ethics, morals and faith rub off on inner-city folks who have never met Jesus." That would happen, he said, as we spent time visiting with them over coffee, helping with their rummage sales, attending their community events, etc. "without any flogging of religion or religious tradition.

"I believe it could be a life-changing experience for them to see you living out your Christian faith," he enthused. "The folks who wanted to be part of our friendship program said they'd like to see how Christianity works.

"Now some detractors of outreach programs like this say the faith you'll be offering these people is just a crutch. Ah, but with encouragement, someone with 'crutch faith' can develop 'walking stick-faith' and then 'pole vault faith!'" he concluded, illustrating his pep talk by leaping off the sanctuary platform.

I signed up enthusiastically as one of the inner-city volunteers our church would send. Motivated, but very young in the Kingdom of God, I plowed zealously, naively into a social situation that required the skill of an experienced Christian social worker.

Dor was the name of the woman I was to befriend. I would visit Dor once a week. I'd meet her family, take her shopping in my car, hear about her life and share about mine. I soon discovered Dor had been inoculated with just enough Christianity to become immune to its life-changing power. She welcomed me into her flat and waited to see how I'd react to its disorganized state. When I passed that test, she introduced me to her lesbian companion and her fatherless child.

Dor let me give her a coat and some casual wear, groceries and advice on meal planning. My effort to help with planning meals on her limited welfare cheque was prompted by realization that money from scavenged pop bottles bought Dor's cigarettes rather than her daughter's school lunches.

Our visits included watching the baseball team she pitched for, attending bingo games she loved and sharing hot dog cookouts in the park with both our families. My husband helped with her furniture when she had to move.

Other than pursuing friendly or practical activities, I never really knew the parameters of my assignment. In my naivety, I kept waiting for Dor to borrow my faith for her "faith crutch". Once that happened, couldn't I expect to see her "crutch" become her "walking stick" and then, marvelously, her "vaulting pole" that would somehow carry her up and away from her present situation?

"Better taught than caught" may be a good maxim, but it wasn't working here. Dor seemed impervious to my version of the Christian faith. I was missing something essential. I didn't expect my lifestyle to become her salvation; I knew better than that. But I struggled with how to share my "crutch of faith" with her.

After my year of visiting was up, Dor moved to yet another location in the inner city. I didn't hear from her again.

When I asked the Lord how I should have handled that opportunity with Dor, He taught me through a missionary visiting from the Far East. He had seen many make the transition from physical and spiritual poverty to joyful, productive life in the Lord. He appreciated the "crutch" theory, agreeing that the witness of a Christian life can motivate interest in Christ, but he assured me that the missing link to successfully planting someone in Christ is introducing them to Jesus as their Savior and Lord.

"Then seekers can lean with all their might on Jesus, not on us", he smiled. "That's the time for us as Christian brothers and sisters to encourage them to move across the ups and downs of life's terrain with their new crutch of faith," he said. "As we share the Bible to teach God's way and strengthen them in understanding and wisdom, then we can watch that crutch turn into a walking stick of faith. Introduce them to the Holy Spirit as the One who empowers believers to leap over life's challenges together with the pole vault of ever-growing faith and we see a lively community of believers born. Finally," he said, "we can expect to see them move out to share that crutch-stick-pole with those who have none."

That sounds like social conscience in action, God's way!

Don't Put Your Glasses On

you don't always have to have everything "just right"

The moment I stepped inside her apartment, Auntie Bee, as everyone called her, took my hand, shook her head and smiled. "Don't put your glasses on, girl," she said. "I haven't had a broom in my hand all week!"

I thought Auntie Bee said that because she knew I try to make sure peace and order in our home helps guests sense the presence of the Holy Spirit.

As a minister's wife in England, Africa and Canada's North, Auntie Bee had met every kind of person you could imagine. And she knew how to love and live with all of them the way Jesus would. While my husband was away for a week-end, I visited with Bee amid her happy, casual disarray and watched as she graciously welcomed into her apartment five unexpected individuals who needed her counsel and ministry over that while. She had, indeed, no time "to pick up a broom".

At the end of our visit, I hugged Auntie Bee goodbye and told her what a lovely time I'd had at her place. She laughed, "You had a lovely time...anyway?"

"No," I smiled, "I had a lovely time...because."

The "because" was the freeing truth I'd learned during that visit with Auntie Bee. Visitors do often comment on the peace and order of our house. But that doesn't mean I must rush to stuff away the newspaper my husband left on the sofa or jam away the laundry I'm folding on the dining room table when a distressed friend arrives unexpectedly on our doorstep, looking for a friendly ear, a prayer partner.

A fun example of this happened one day when we had just finished a big stew supper. We answered the door bell to find two dinner guests (expected the following week) standing there smiling, apologizing for being late.

It was on the tip of my tongue to say, "You're not late, just a week early!" Grace was mine in that moment: I didn't.

"Like Bee," whispered the Holy Spirit and I rejoiced as we seated our friends in the living room with a glass of apple cider without a thought about the before-cleaning-day condition of our home. I plugged in the kettle to make a big batch of hot, steaming pasta with choice of tomato or cream sauce (both canned). A dish of celery sticks and olives followed by ice cream and cookies completed the work of my own fast food kitchen that night.

I smiled, noting the heaping portions my husband piled high for our friends and the minuscule servings he served the two of us. I reminded myself to laud him for his good humor and discretion after our guests would leave.

As we took after-dinner coffee in the living room, our friends asked for our input about an unwelcome situation they would be facing the following week. Did we give them the fine dinner and entertainment we had planned for them the next week? No, but we were available to talk and pray their problem through with them when they needed our help as their brother and sister in the Lord.

Was the house perfect? Umm, hardly. Was the meal to sigh over? No. Did they see the pile of laundry I kicked under the sideboard? Hope not. The important thing was that they needed friends to agree in prayer with them that they might hear what God wanted to do as the day of their challenge drew near. The Lord had us there to pray with them. The "wrong night" they came proved to be the right night after all.

Indeed, it was a good time ..."because".

A thought: wouldn't it be great to grind underfoot those spectacles of "flesh" that have us seeing earthly matters as being so all-important? If we keep perched on our noses the spiritual specs Jesus gives us to see life as He sees it, we can evaluate what's important as we discern the needs and hurts the Lord wants us to tend in His Name.

We don't know the needs that might arrive with friends on the doorstep, any minute, any day, but the Lord does.

And yes, I try to make sure His peace and order of my home is always there even if the dishes are still in the sink!

Spiritual Memos

the Holy Spirit's prayer promptings

Why should this story trigger memories of that old friend? Why should this dessert have me thinking about that relative? Why should this radio show bring that friend to mind?

The answer to such questions can come with an unexpected phone call from someone who has come to mind. Hearing from that person on the phone usually prompts my genuine exclamation, "But I was just thinking about you!"

It's happened to me enough times now, that I almost expect to hear a friend say, "Well I hope you were praying for me." Then, he or she will begin to share a problem or situation that was being experienced when the Lord brought that one to my mind.

For Christian believers of Holy Spirit-led prayer, such a "prompting" is not a fluke of memory or an impromptu triggering of some psychological signal. It might be a call to prayer if we have chosen to keep our minds and hearts open to His prompting. Sometimes signals for prayer action seem designed to capture our attention when we are doing anything but looking for things to pray about.

When applying eye-make-up, I have occasionally thought of a friend who returned to her home in Egypt a number of years ago. We had enjoyed many hours studying the Bible together. One day she taught me how to use...guess what? Eye-liner! We lost touch after she left and I've had no news about her for years. But I choose to pray that she may have God's strength, comfort and wisdom when I'm prompted to remember this gracious sister in the Lord. When we meet again in Heaven one day, I can expect to hear what was going on at the time I was remembering her!

Spiritual memos can play a part in The Holy Spirit's awesome communications system...awesome in the real sense of that word. We just have to be alert to pick up the signals and go to prayer for the safety, health, encouragement, effectiveness, wisdom or whatever seems appropriate when the Holy Spirit brings to mind people for whom God has given us concern.

Sharing: Partnering With The Holy Spirit

pointing up and away

Something was out of whack with our new weekly Bible study group.

When we started, it seemed we were all in the same boat as new and young Christians, eager to grow in our faith, study the Gospel of John and share what we were learning. But after the first few meetings, I was uncomfortable.

As an enquiring pre-Christian, the thought of witnessing had intimidated me. But after accepting Jesus as my Savior I determined to not only study, but to also live the Gospels, even if that meant witnessing to other people about what the Lord was doing in my life.

The Holy Spirit opened up to me a new, wonderful world as I pored and prayed over the Gospels. I wanted His help to put what I was learning into practice. I was eager to share my adventures with God and looked for others to do the same.

These things we speak not in words which man's wisdom teaches, but which the Holy Spirit teaches, comparing spiritual things with spiritual (1 Corinthians 2:13).

But when I shared with my new study group, they only listened. They didn't share their experiences. Why? What was

I doing wrong? Did I open my mouth too often? Did others think I fancied myself a teacher? I was no teacher. I was a learner, a novice like everyone else in the group.

Then some of the group began looking to me for answers to bumps and potholes they ran into on their new walk with the Lord, instead of checking with their Bibles, the pastor or a more experienced Christian than I. I wasn't comfortable with that.

This was one of those times to get alone with the Lord and ask, "What's up, Lord?"

As I asked, the Lord responded, "Let's start with why the things I've taught you embarrass you."

"Oh, Lord, I could never be embarrassed about anything You teach me," I said. "But I am uncomfortable at being seen as someone with lots of answers when I've only learned enough to know I need to learn a whole lot more!"

"Then perhaps you're concerned about the lack of response when you share," He nudged me.

"That must be it," I said. "Anything I learn from Your Word or hear from Your Holy Spirit is a gift I want to share. But it's when sharing results in people regarding me as some teacher with answers that I squirm."

"If reaction to your sharing makes you squirm, what about the way you share?" the Holy Spirit said, stressing the word, "way".

I could tell He wanted me to work this through. Well, I thought, I want to do things the way Jesus did. So how did Jesus reach people? When He talked to them, He was always pointing to God.

"Yes!" I laughed in that eureka moment, "if I share the way Jesus did, I won't worry about people looking to me for answers. They'll be looking up to God the Father, Son and Holy Spirit!"

"Okay, Holy Spirit!" I said, feeling full of enthusiastic exclamation marks, "I'm signing on as one of your junior partners whenever I go to share with anybody, anywhere, at anytime!"

At Bible study that night I prayed as the study began, "Lord, please help us, each one, to share what we're learning the way You want it shared. Help us encourage people the way You want them encouraged. We want our witness centred on You as the one who blesses, leads and teaches. Together, we want to lift Jesus high for all those around us to see!"

After exploring together our need for God's direction in everything we did, including witnessing, each of us specifically asked for His guidance to witness to His Way, in His way.

As the months passed we became a hive of sharers pointing out to anyone interested, the way God was changing our lives. The honey we spread attracted new members who joined us to begin their own relationship with Jesus, dig into the Gospel of John we were studying and share their own testimonies. Every word pointed to Jesus, the sweet centre of this new life in Christ. Someone at church nicknamed us, "The Busy Bees".

"That's good," one member of our study group laughed, "as long as we remember who the "Keeper" is!"

_____

Bridge People

when they're on the scene, division doesn't have a chance

Bridge People aren't all that obvious. They promote their work, not themselves.

Bridge People gravitate to scenes of action where Satan is wielding his favorite tool: division. Few tools give him as much pleasure. His intention is to divide God's people so they can't pull together to effect the plans God has given them.

Bridge People have a quiet hand in the work of peacemaking, reconciling, mending, healing and encouraging, but they don't hesitate to give God the credit if the spotlight finds them.

The spotlight usually finds them when they challenge attitudes and motives that promote self-interest and divisiveness. Combatants in the heat of battle rarely appreciate them, but Bridge People don't become peacemakers to win popularity.

Satan doesn't see Bridge People coming. He can't spot them when their eyes are fixed on Jesus and those they help for Him, because they look so much like Jesus! Nor does he see them working, as their quick, quiet steps evidence Jesus, not self.

Bridge People's discerning eyes, perceptive minds and insightful actions operate for one objective: to reconcile what Satan would pull apart and what God would bring and keep together. Conciliators in the world help bridge opposition by helping disparate parties reach a compromise. But Bridge People of the Lord, in the power of the Holy Spirit, do the ultimate in restoration as they carry on the work of the greatest Bridge and Bridge Builder of all, Jesus. When He lay down His life He bridged the sin chasm between God and man that "whosoever will" (John 3:15) might safely cross to the arms of His love and power.

Bridge People enjoy the anonymity they usually work under, as they lift up Jesus that He may draw all men to Himself (John 12:32). They let their works shine before men for one reason: to glorify God (Matthew 5:16).

You could call Bridge People "God's undercover agents". That's the way they like it!

A Tough Assignment

a stubborn friend says she wants help but won't take it

I sink back into my favorite armchair, prop up my feet and let out a sigh.

"Ah, peace," I'm thinking. "It's over: the confrontation, the fighting against deception in that stubborn woman, trying to show her what's really going on in her life. She asks for help and then doesn't listen to anything I have to say.

"All that time and energy spent for nothing. I'm out of this battle. I'm putting it behind me. I may still be a young Christian at this point, and just trying to help, but I can tell when my peace is broken. But here, now, with this confrontation aside, I can have my peace again."

"And is it My peace that passes all understanding?" (Philippians 4:7).

I recognize the voice of the Holy Spirit, provoking my thought because He wants to lead my thinking.

"I guess if it's not peace, at least the stress is less," I reason. "The tension headache is gone. Tomorrow I won't wake up with this on my mind. I can tackle some of the things I've put on hold since she asked for my help.

"But there was a moment, there," I speculate, "when she seemed to soften her stand. I thought she was going to be more receptive as I offered my help this time. But then she clamped her jaw tight again and was every bit as stubborn as she was last time she was going through this problem."

"What was your response when she once more balked at your help?" The Holy Spirit prods my thinking.

"I was tired of the hassle by then," I say. "I guess I told her she could do whatever she thought best, never mind what

I thought, even though she'd asked for my input. But Lord, how much do I have to take? How long can I keep turning myself inside out for her?"

"Inside out, you say? Does that sound like ministering in the spirit"? the Holy Spirit asks, beckoning me along the path of His thoughts. "Even as she became a victim of the deceiver (Revelation 12:9), you yourself have now fallen prey to his devices (Matthew 7:15). You believe because she won't listen, you can't help. Are you seeing her situation as a burden you want to drop?

"Doing battle in the flesh what can only be done in the spirit is always burdensome. That should indicate to you that your flesh has been in control. If the devil can convince you to back off, he's succeeded in what he was aiming to do. Once that is done, he'll underline your resolve to stay out of this by pretending to ease his harassment of your friend.

"But it will be a false peace; her dilemma is not yet dealt with. Once you drop your concern for her, he'll gear up his program for her harassment. But you are the Spirit-filled friend of prayer she called on. So stay alert (1 Peter 5:8), remember Proverbs 15:28 and study how to answer.

"My ministry for this stubborn child still awaits her. Can you submit your frustration to Me and once more be available to bring her to Me in prayer to ask for the grace that she needs so desperately?"

I sprint for the phone, enthusiasm* renewed, then pause before dialing my friend's number to beg, "O, Holy Spirit, please keep that crack in the door of her heart open while I...I mean 'we'...reach out to her again. If I'm following hard after You, I know I'll have the words to convince her to bring this mess to You. And together, we'll come before You on wings of prayer! Then we'll see what the Lord will do!"

* enthusiasm: from Greek entheos = en theos = in God

Computer, Holy Spirit Style

the Holy Spirit has the best "prompts"

I was imagining my brain as computer under the control of the Lord. After all, if Creator God made this universe in which all the laws of physics can be illustrated, couldn't we say He is the first and best physicist?

The idea of my brain as a computer with the Lord at the controls, moving the "mouse" where He wills, brings the subject of listening to God into the parable category. Although I've been having fun with this idea, it does give a new appreciation of what it can mean to give access to our thinking for the Holy Spirit's use anytime, anywhere.

Just as my grandsons can listen to music while operating their computers, I can make a meal and pray for my friend who is about to have her baby. Step that up to the next level. I am making the meal, praying for my friend about to have her baby and the thought comes, "Give Phil that funny Bill Cosby book, Time Flies".

I wasn't thinking about Phil and his retirement. I haven't heard from the Grants since his wife accepted my fruit plate offer for his retirement party. Nor is my idea provoked by the sight of Bill Cosby's book. But I believe the Lord can bring to mind the needs of people we know, encouraging us to apply the "program" of thoughtfulness He would have us apply to our relationships.

Believers, who deliberately give the Holy Spirit access to their hearts, minds and wills anytime He wants to make use of them, become used to His thoughts being dropped among their thoughts. It's just surprising the way He does it sometimes. He knows the working of our computers (brains) better than we do and operates them in any mode at anytime if we choose to listen for Him.

Back to the meal I was putting together: it turned out well. My guests didn't leave a crumb. My friend did have an easy birth and a healthy baby. Phil did get the book and the friendly levity on the topic of retirement softened some sharp edges of his pre-retirement jitters.

Analogies can only go so far to make a point. But this little incident of Holy Spirit input is an example of how God loves to prompt our response to situations that need both prayer and action. Perhaps we can take the analogy far enough to say, "Lord, keep your hand on the Holy Spirit keyboard and we'll stay online for Your input."

God Who?

the wrong "lord" wanted to keep her from her Lord

During our teen years she'd been only a little shorter than I. But at this moment, in that big bed, she looked small and fragile. I was spending my regular day with my friend Ann that last summer of her life. Cancer was ravaging her body, but it couldn't touch her quick wit or beautiful smile.

"Sit down on the bed here beside me," she said. "Tell me what's happening in that interesting life of yours. And I have some news for you and some questions too."

In our teens I'd always looked up to "big sister" Ann, as the most intelligent, attractive, charming girl I knew. I was always the one asking Ann questions. Now she was saying she had questions for me. This day there was a sense of expectancy in the air that I didn't get an immediate fix on.

"Lord," I prayed under my breath, "You see it from beginning to end. You lead. I'll follow."

Even while I was sharing the happenings of my week with Ann, I was thinking how dramatically our relationship had changed after we'd headed to university. When we both married, we almost drifted apart as our common ground developed furrows of different outlooks, attitudes and preferences. As our young families visited in those early days, a distinct alienation between our interests, passions and purposes began to show up. And then there was the mockery.

The mockery came when her husband Phil grabbed the opportunity to make snide remarks whenever anything about our new life in Christ came up. And it did come up. When Jesus is your life, He's a natural part of your conversation. I was devastated as Ann looked on with amusement when Phil would mock any reference to the Lord.

When my husband and I took it to the Lord in prayer, He told us to just keep on loving them. "They don't understand. Go ahead and live your life in Me in front of them. My grace is there for the mockery and insults. Let those pass over your heads; they will not affect you. Be on the watch for where I will lead you, that you won't miss any turns!"

We did experience God's grace and Phil's clever, searing remarks did pass over our heads without effect. And that was true of our kids as well. Passionate about their relationship with Jesus and the people He brought into their lives, they looked forward to our times with Phil and Ann's family. They accepted the way they were and loved them for Jesus no matter what.

During one of those family visits Ann read an article I'd written for a Christian publication and asked me about my own relationship with Jesus and His people that obviously meant so much to me. That encouraged me until a mutual friend told me to watch what I told Ann. On coffee breaks together Ann often made fun of what I had shared with her.

When I asked the Lord about this, He gave me the same admonition as before: to just keep on loving them. I thought, "I'll do that until God tells me something more."

Those Tuesday visits that last summer with Ann were precious. Of course, Jesus was as natural a part of my conversation as ever. Ann's response, indicating a curiosity about life in Christ, never suggested she was interested in trying it for herself.

"Lord?" I asked Him after a visit marked by a sudden barrage of her questions, "When she keeps asking such imperative questions, why can she not respond to my answers?"

I wasn't expecting His answer: "Her husband is her god."

With that truth echoing in my mind, I prayed silently as I sat beside her that last week of her life. "Lord, I believe You'd have me bind the influence of that idol in her life. So standing on Matthew 16:19, in the Name of Jesus, I do!"

The questions Ann had wanted to ask me on our last visit were thoughtful, moving. She wanted to hear about the life that starts with Christ here and now and continues after death. They were especially poignant in light of her news about the doctor's last report. It said her death was imminent, probably before the end of the month. I remember few details of this final time of sharing. But I do remember that she asked a question that could only be answered by introducing her to Jesus as Savior and Lord.

Ann prayed with her whole heart to receive Jesus into her life. Together we cried joyful tears and embraced: two sisters in Christ at last.

When Phil came home from work he was surprised to see my car in the driveway. "Nan, you're still here! Where ever did you leave my dinner?" he called up the stairs.

"Come see," I laughed. "You sweethearts deserve a fancy dinner together. It's set up here tonight."

He bounded up the stairs, kissed his wife and grinned at dinner spread out with lace and best dinnerware, hers on a bedside tray, his on a small table nearby.

When Phil let out a salacious remark (his way to compliment a woman) it went in my one ear and out the other as usual.

But this time it was different for Ann. No chuckle, no little smile. She raised her frail self on her poor thin arms and said in a no-nonsense tone, "Don't ever speak to Nan like that again."

I was quiet as I went downstairs to take up the meal for Ann and Phil. But inside bells were ringing: Phil's no longer her god! God is!

I stayed to clean up the kitchen and was blessed by the happy chatter coming from the bedroom above.

Ann died the next week with Phil by her bedside, holding her hand.

Phil was committed to the hospital himself with a fast-moving cancer close to the first anniversary of Ann's death. He told me he was prepared to follow his sweetheart; the sooner the better, as life had been so empty without her. Days later, a friend, who was a professional colleague, prayed with Phil to accept Jesus as his Lord and Savior.

It sounded like a fairy tale where two sweethearts are united again in death. But it was no fairy tale. It was a true story of God's love triumphing, as friends were obedient to share with them the Good News of Christ.

In the next few years it was suspected, from the high incidence of cancer deaths on the little cul-de-sac where they had lived, that the street might have been built on contaminated soil. Literally, Phil and Ann had been taken out of a cancerous pit and lifted to the highest ground of God's love and mercy.

God has taught me to share the love and life of Jesus wherever and whenever He says. Because He promises believers, in Matthew 17:10, that whatever we bind on earth will be bound in heaven and whatever we loose on earth will be loosed in heaven, we can bind the hindrances that Satan would try to use to stop someone from considering life with Christ and accepting Him as Savior and Lord.

Constantly amazed at the way God-plans work out, I love telling Phil and Ann's story. It shows again, our part in simply listening and following what Jesus tells us to do.

The blessing of The Lord makes rich and He adds no sorrow with it (Proverbs 10:22).

Not Me And My Shadow

not a worm turning, but a friend being a real friend

Like a shadow, she walked in sync with me whenever we went anywhere together, never differing in opinion, never disagreeing. It might have seemed flattering, but I was starting to wonder if this was the way a friendship in Christ was supposed to be.

While I was a young Christian myself, I understood that though Audrey might follow a mentor's thoughts and ways for a while, she had her own walk to walk with Jesus. I had been asked to take her under my wing to help her do just that. The pastor who had prayed with her as she had renewed her life in the Lord, had encouraged me that it wouldn't be hard to help someone who had made such a genuine u-turn in her life.

Audrey and I had spent quality time securing the spiritual foundation stones such as prayer and Bible study in her Christian life. Her eagerness to learn and apply what she was learning was evident, but her "shadow personality" didn't seem to be a good sign.

"I have an unsettled feeling about this, Lord," I told Him. "I don't think I'm old enough in this lamb-tending business to identify what's out of kilter here."

"Her focus," came His succinct reply.

Her focus? I thought. Despite my good intentions to disciple her to Jesus, had she become focused on my walk rather than on the Person with whom I walk? I didn't want to come between her and her personal walk with the Lord and I spent some earnest moments in prayer over the matter.

When I asked the Lord how I could redirect her focus, without seeming to put down her steadfast efforts to walk a Christian walk, His simple reply was, "Talk about it."

Audrey and I were able to comfortably discuss God's use of friends for our growth through their example, not their control. It was liberating to tell her, "I'll be delighted, not offended, to see you mercilessly scrutinize everything I say, to see how it lines up with Scripture!"

In the months ahead, we grew to relate more as big and little sister than as teacher and pupil. The change became obvious the day we were driving home from a particularly stimulating women's meeting. The Christian speaker had sparked lively small group involvement, the kind of discussion we both loved.

I waited for her keen observations that evidenced her growing reliance on Jesus.

This time she was quiet...the kind of quiet that can indicate a reluctance to say something. My encouragement finally drew her out to share, and what a sharing it was!

"I could feel disloyal for thinking like this," she began, a little fiercely, "because you've been a good friend to me. I've learned a lot of biblical principles from you. You make them real so I can make them real for myself.

"But it's because of the very things you've taught me that I have to say this to your face: why do you use people's names when you're sharing? You can believe I want to see God get credit for changes He's made in me. But now I'm wondering after listening to you share tonight if you would show how God can work in someone's life, by using my story with my name. It scares me and it isn't right! It amounts to gossip."

I was floored. Of course it wasn't right. I had indeed unwittingly engaged is a form of gossip. I agreed with her. Such poor discipline of my tongue could not have pleased Jesus at all.

She relaxed when I received her charge to me as coming from the Lord through her intervention, and we both regained our peace as we took the matter to Him in prayer.

The Lord's compassion poured through my friend at my contrition. She forgave me and stood by me as I asked God's forgiveness and renounced that awful tendency. Both her admonition and prayer for me were thorough, heartfelt and have proven effective to this day, many years later.

Audrey had come out of the shadow into the sunshine of relationship with God in a new way. My little sister had grown up, blessed me and begun her own walk to help others who want to grow in Him.

To The Friend I Failed

God refocuses our prayers for His purpose.

Can a Christian fail a friend who needs help? Watching a dear friend struggling with her grief after we'd spent hours sharing and praying together, I saw how little I'd really helped. Confused and disappointed as her heartache continued to grow, I looked to the Lord for His plans to replace mine and then wrote her this letter.

Dear Carol,

I thought about your pain long and hard today, of all you've been through in these past months and how much I've wanted to help. I may have been there for you, but today as I was talking with the Lord, I saw how little I've been able to do for you. I've been standing, as it were, with the hands of my spirit hanging at my sides, useless. I wanted so much to save you from your pain. I wanted to take on your sorrow. But all I did was come under your pain myself. Your pain had become my pain and my soul couldn't bear it.

"Why does this wound stay so open, Lord?" I asked. "You are the God of so many rescues in my own life. Why do the life jackets I pitch into my friend's hurt and sorrow float uselessly away? Dear Lord, how, why have I failed her?"

"My child," He answered, "you know that it's not in you to heal except by My Spirit."

The simple truth struck me like a ten-ton truck. I was identifying so deeply with your pain over the loss of the husband you've loved so much that I'd lost my perspective. My friend, I was so caught up in my own need to help, that if I could have done it, I would have picked up your grief like a backpack and strapped it to myself. The Lord's answer had not condemned me for wanting to help but did convict me of being presumptuous.

The Lord was calling me to be a prayer warrior for you, not a sponge for your pain. Instead of turning with you to His Holy Spirit to minister His peace and healing to your grieving soul, I was busy being your sacrificing friend, determined to carry your hurt myself.

I do know the pain of losing a loved one. I too have experienced the vacant place a dear one can leave in one's life. I can identify with what you are going through. Surely if Romans 12:15 teaches me to weep with those who weep and Matthew 22:30 says I am to love my neighbor as myself, I've done that. But I know I was never meant to bear your pain myself. Jesus has done that already on the cross.

Believers are equipped to be His agents of help only by His Holy Spirit and to pray for peace, comfort and healing only in Jesus' name. To forget that is to fail to help the suffering friends we care for.

May God release you from the anxiety I've smothered you with these past months as I ask forgiveness of both you and our Lord. No matter how well-meaning I could be, the Lord could never use my anxiety to heal your broken heart. But He will use my faith in His power to do that.

As we have done before, let's plan to "come boldly to the throne of grace, that we may obtain mercy and find grace to help in time of need," as Hebrews 4:16 tells us. This time, when we finish praying, I won't pick you up and carry you out of that place of prayer on my back, as it were. This time, I'll leave you in the hands of Jesus, who mends hearts in a way no one else can do.

I love you, Carol. You'll continue to hear often from me as I look to the Lord for how He wants me to pray as well as for practical ways I can help. Practical help is another way the Holy Spirit equips us and He's such a good tutor!

- Nan

You did not choose Me, but I chose you and appointed you that you should go and bear fruit, and that your fruit should remain, that whatever you ask the Father in My Name, He may give you. These things I command you, that you love one another (John 14: 16, 17).

God is able to do exceedingly abundantly above all that we ask or think, according to His power that works in us (Ephesians 3:20).

When We All Get Together Up There

looking past the curtain that divides

Dear Amy,

So sorry about your Mom's death. I know something of the difficult time you're going through. My dad died of a heart attack at 49, when I was 18. Some friends said, "Oh it's so much worse when a loved one has a prolonged dying." But I knew better. I'd lost Grandma two months before from a long bout with cancer. It's hard to lose a loved one at any time.

Besides being hard, the unexpected loss of your Mom must also be bewildering. I know how bewildering such a sudden tragedy can be. My sister and I were both attending university. Our folks had just sold our house and were packing up to move the four of us in with Dad's 90-year-old mother until he (an engineer) had overseen the building of their new house on three beautiful, wooded acres. Mom and Dad were on the verge of a brand new life on that acreage. We two sisters were planning our weddings that would start our own new lives after graduation. But the day the truck was to move us to Grandma's was the day Dad's heart stopped and life changed dramatically.

Some friends said, "Your dad's death was God's plan. He knows best!"

But I was sure God's plans must be for good and this certainly wasn't good. If bad things happened to us or our loved ones, we had to believe in the existence of a good God who cared and would help us through those bad places.

That painful time came before I met Jesus. Though I didn't yet know God personally, I had appreciated everything I'd heard about Him. Though I didn't yet know to listen for His comfort and guidance through His Spirit and His Word, I walked through that difficult time with a certain peace and an assurance that a caring God was watching over me. I never questioned my expectation that good things lay ahead for my future.

During the weeks and months that followed, my sister and I were so busy holding Mom up emotionally, that we shelved our own personal grief. When I finally collapsed in a heap of tears one evening about six months later, my fiancé, Bill, was there to see me through the built-up grief as your Peter has been for you.

Six years later when I accepted Jesus into my life and gave Him my heart, the loss of my Dad came vividly to mind. The memory came with an inner peace that seemed to reassure me that the Lord had been with me through my grief, even more than my dear Bill had been.

I was so excited when I found the Scripture that underlined the truth I had experienced those six years before, that I memorized it:

"For I know the thoughts I think toward you," says the Lord, "thoughts of peace and not of evil, to give you a future and a hope. Then you will call upon Me and go and pray to Me, and I will listen to you. And you will seek Me and find Me when you search for Me with all your heart" (Jeremiah 29:11-13).

Memories of loved ones are special and will last until we are reunited with them in Heaven. Then we won't have to grab the snapshot albums to look for a dear one's face or listen to a tape of a beloved's voice, or touch a well-worn garment to feel close to the one who has left us. On the day we see Jesus face-to-face and meet our loved ones again, we can delight in shared greetings, embraces and reminiscences as though we had never been parted.

Amy, you are one who is always helping others. I can see you bearing up under your own sorrow to give comfort to your Mother's other loved ones. But Jesus doesn't just pat the hands of caregivers. He doesn't just commiserate with our pain as we reach out to others who grieve. He who took our pain on Himself on the cross, now folds us in His arms to give us His healing. He's there through our painful times, as no one else can be. He blesses you to be the blessing your Mom knew you to be. You can rest and abide in that love, Amy, just like your Mom is doing right now!

God bless you Amy. You are in my prayers. Your friend, Nan.

Rejection? Hand Me My Spiritual Specs!

not taking any more guff from the enemy

I know people, who like I used to do, live on a level lower than God ever intended until they realize they really are "accepted in the Beloved" (Ephesians 1:6). Take Sally for example.

I would often tell my young Christian friend when she faced rejection to remember God saw her as made righteous in Christ, as no longer under condemnation. When Satan tried to pull her down with rejection, she could put on her spiritual spectacles, so to speak, and see herself as God saw her.

This day, the phone at my ear was percolating with her laughter and I knew a good report was on its way. Christian sisters, Sally and I are committed to the rebuilding of her soul from rejection that had badly damaged her self-image. Now that she is in Christ, His Holy Spirit is working on her understanding of identity in Him.

Sally began her story with the realization that the woman she'd just met had taken an instant dislike to her. After checking out her own behavior for any unintentional offense she might have given, Sally braved the woman's frigid manner to directly but graciously ask if she had somehow offended her.

At Sally's gentle concern, the woman burst into tears and shared with her the pain of rejection that was always with her and had fostered the curt, aloof way she treated people, even as she had treated Sally.

Recognizing a God-opportunity, Sally seized it with her growing confidence in Christ. She listened to the woman's story, shared what the Lord had taught her about dealing with a spirit of rejection and offered to pray for her.

"I told her we were in the same boat," chortled Sally over the phone. "And because I refused Satan the right to be the coxswain calling our strokes, we'd make it safe to shore," she waxed eloquent in her excitement.

The woman knew about Jesus, Sally told me, but didn't have a personal relationship with Him. Sally had pulled out her pocket New Testament and opened it to Hebrews 13:8 to read, "Jesus Christ (is) the same yesterday, today and forever."

"I told her He wants us to walk with Him, expecting great things and accepting His strength for our weaknesses. I read Acts 10:15 to her about not calling ourselves unworthy because Jesus has redeemed us. I told her just how much like her I'd been and when I gave her one of my favorite sayings from Bible teacher Bill Gothard, 'Please be patient, God isn't finished with me yet', she smiled a little bit. Then I showed her 2 Corinthians 1:4 about comforting others with the comfort He's comforted us with and she broke out with a big smile to say, 'And that's just what you're doing with me right now, isn't it?'

"If you'd been there to hear what I said then," she laughed, "you'd know I'm not taking any more guff from Satan. I told her, 'I've been where you are, but you aren't going to stay there anymore than I did if Jesus has anything to do with it!'

"The woman started laughing with me through her tears and we exchanged phone numbers. I'll be hearing from her, you can bet!"

As she hung up, her joy stayed with me. Satan had missed Sally by a mile this time. Because she acted on the Word of God instead of falling under apparent condemnation, she was now carrying more equipment in her spiritual arsenal that she's ever known before and she's going to use it.

Casting Your Burden Where It Belongs
"burn out" is an alert

Whenever you meet a passionate Christian you get some good tips to put in your "empowerment" file.

We met such a Christian at a Full Gospel Businessmen's Breakfast meeting when a smiling, affable man approached the book table where my husband and I were helping.

"Learned a lot from Christian books," Ron said looking over the book display, "but experiences serving the Lord have taught me more than any book I've ever read, except the Bible."

"Oh," I said, always ready to hear and record a good story, "we'd love to hear about some of those lessons, if you'd like to go for coffee after we close up."

"Do you know what you're getting into?" he laughed, "I have a reputation as a talker, you know!"

Ron lived up to his reputation and we enjoyed every minute of his animated sharing as he regaled us with his "God adventures" over coffee. Our respect grew as he shared his failures as well as his victories for the Lord.

We won't forget one particularly affecting story Ron told us. It was how he learned to handle the depression he experienced whenever the Gospel message he shared with a dying man fell on defiant ears.

—⚬·⚬—

Ron's story

Every Christian who means business with God, gets an assignment. My specific assignment is to visit men dying in the hospital who've never heard the Gospel. I go, knowing it's their last chance to hear. And I go, knowing He loves every one of them, even the difficult ones.

Some of the difficult ones are suffering the consequences of wrong living in their bodies. Some fear the future because they've lived evil lives. Some hold hard-as-rock defiance towards God. And I go, knowing for sure that God sends me there because He always gives me a specific message for each man, even though I may not know the details of his life. But always, always, I know that man needs to hear about God's love for him.

I've seen many dying men take first steps towards Christ during my hospital visits and I've left their rooms walking on clouds, rejoicing.

But sometimes I've left a man's room with a heavy heart when a "tough love" word God has given me to speak has been rejected. One man turned his back on me, another ordered me from his room, and another refused to speak further with me.

If God says His yoke is easy and His burden light (Matthew 11:30) how can a Christian, looking to God for His empowerment to do what He's told him to do, experience "burn out"? But I was facing it.

"Lord," I groaned, driving home after one of those heart-wrenching visits, "I'm not complaining, but I wonder at times why You tell me to come on so strong. Some of these men get mad when I'm blunt and this depression moves right in on me.

"I want to be firm, kind and honest with those who let me share about Jesus, God's love and the Life Hereafter. The men who accept Christ often tell me I made the message easy to consider. That's what I want to see: Your Holy Spirit wooing people as I share Your Word. I'm going to tell them about Your love and nothing's going to stop me. But what can I do about the depression that hits every time I share with men who get angry at the mention of Your Name?

"I'm sure Satan has a claim on the lives of defiant men and tries to thwart any effort to get them through Heaven's Gate. I'm also sure it's crucial for any warrior heading into spiritual battle to follow biblical warning to put on the whole armor of God and bind the enemy's work (Ephesians 6:11-17, Matthew 16:19, 18:18).

"I use those scriptures every time I approach a dying man who doesn't know You want him in heaven, not hell. I know angels rejoice in heaven if he receives that message, but depression grips me if he rejects it.

"Lord, the man I just left...I can still see the hate on his face as he grabbed my Bible and threw it on the hospital floor at the mention of Your Name."

Trying to drive home after that scene, needing peace to hear from God, I pulled the car to the side of the road. I leaned on the steering wheel, staring out the window in front of me but seeing nothing...and seeing nothing in the Spirit either.

As I prayed in the spirit, begging for understanding, the Holy Spirit quickened to me another "burden" scripture: "Cast your burden on the Lord, and He shall sustain you; He shall never permit the righteous to be moved" (Psalm 55:22).

As the words refreshed my spirit, I could see the source of my confusion and pain. The burden for souls starts with Jesus. He asks us to share His burden, to tell people about His love and His plans for their lives. But whether someone obediently sharing the Gospel likes it or not, God gives men free will to reject or accept Him.

A man's decision is his own to make. When he has, no matter which way that decision goes, the burden God gives me for him is no longer mine to carry. I can cast my burden on the Lord knowing I've shared what God told me even as I know I must accept a man's right to reject Jesus. But how I rejoice as I return to God the burden for any man if that man has welcomed Jesus into his life!

_⸰⸰_

Ron finished his story and after a moment said quietly, "If I feel bad when a dying man refuses Jesus, think how God must feel when His love is rejected. He loved us so much He sacrificed His Son to bridge the sin gap between God and us. Oh, that dying men might know... I have to go to see them. If they're going to have a last chance to decide, they have to hear."

_⸰⸰_

Help! I Flip-Flopped Again

learning to stay consistent in Christ

Our son's friend, Dan, came to our side door with a troubled teenager from his class at school. Her name was Lannie. She had decided to leave home and had nowhere to go. Since ours was a Christian home, he thought she might stay with us for a while.

I was glad Dan realized our Christian home would be open to someone who needed help. When our son Larry had brought his highly intellectual school chum home to hear about Jesus the week before, we weren't quite sure what his reaction to the Gospel had been. Dan had listened thoughtfully, thanked us and then said he'd have to think about it.

He didn't get back to us and had said nothing further to Larry. Yet here he was today with someone in tow who needed help. He must have gathered that Christians are caring people. Lannie, he explained, was a druggie. She was at odds with her indifferent mother and bent on leaving home.

We said she could stay with us for a while if she thought it could help her and if she got her mother's permission.

On hearing this, Dan pressed Lanni in my direction, bowed and turned to leave, calling over his shoulder as he did, "May it go well!"

I watched and left Dan in the Lord's hands as he made his way down our driveway to the street. We've never seen him since, but I prayed that night that God would bless the seed we'd planted there and bring Dan to Himself, making use of that wonderful brain and gentle heart for His Kingdom.

That night after supper, Lannie helped with the dishes and then phoned her mother for permission to stay with us a couple of months until school started in September.

"Well, I guess I got permission. She just said, 'Sure, why not?' and hung up. She couldn't have cared less," Lannie whispered, looking at the floor.

Over the next two months, Lannie accepted our moral support to kick drugs. Her confidence heightened when she became an enthusiastic Christian and she set her sights on "going back home to win Mom to the Lord!"

Our son and daughter who had spent much time with our young house guest were as concerned as I about Lannie's apparently impetuous plan. We spent the next week talking and praying with Lannie, Bible in hand, suggesting it would be wise to give herself a bit more time to practise her new walk with Jesus before returning home. Undaunted, Lannie hugged us all, thanked us for our hospitality and for introducing her to Jesus and went home.

Within the week, she phoned to exclaim, "Oh Nan, I flip-flopped!"

She shared how her mother had baited her, laughed at her "religion" and provoked her into a shouting match. "I got so emotional. I couldn't get my spirit back in control," she cried.

"You're not alone, Lannie" I said gently. "We all fight that battle at times. The temptation to let our emotions take over is something we all face. But our souls, your soul Lannie, they're beautiful when our spirits are ruling them. If Satan tries to distract us with shock or anger, he's doing it to provoke us and he aims at our weak areas. You just have to start praising God the instant you see the provocation starting to take place."

"But I was so angry I couldn't remember one praise song" she whimpered. "Oh, I've made a mess of everything."

"Well, one day not long ago, Lannie," I said, "you learned to use your spiritual language anytime you get confused, upset or angry," I reminded her.

"Yah, I did, didn't I?" Lannie said in a more relaxed tone as she recalled that time when she had asked Jesus to fill her with His Holy Spirit. "I got my spiritual language when I was baptized in the Holy Spirit that night in your living room with all you guys there, praying for me."

"You sure did!" I laughed. "When your flesh is unruly and disconnected from the Lord, you can let your spiritual language loose in praise. Soon you're sensing His peace and wisdom and you know your spirit's back in control. Once again, you have the grace you need to do what the Holy Spirit would have you do."

"But my soul isn't always so bad, is it, Nan?" Lannie said, "Isn't Christ's life in me now?"

"Oh, Lannie dear, of course!" I said. "But your direction has to come from your spirit, submitted to Jesus' Holy Spirit in you, if you're to hear how the Lord wants to lead you. You do remember, don't you?"

"Yes," she whispered. "Forgive me, Nan?"

"Lannie, it's not from me you need to ask forgiveness. Ask the Lord for that. Ask that His Holy Spirit give you a nudge when you forget to stay close to Him. Ask that His Holy Spirit take charge again so you can speak and do as Jesus would."

"Yeah, the Jesus Way. That's what I want," she said. "Thanks for the re-direct, Nan."

Then a giggle over the phone: "I've got my hand stuck out in front of me, like you used to show me. My spirit, like my thumb that is turned down, pointing to the floor, here, has been pushed to the bottom all week. But as I praise the Lord, my spirit's going to get back into its place of authority with the Holy Spirit. So now my spirit, just like my thumb has flipped back into top position just where it's supposed to be. In control of my soul, my spirit is again pointing straight to heaven.

"My three middle fingers here, are lined up together beneath my thumb. They're like the three parts of my soul, right? My mind, my will and my emotions. They're supposed to stay like that, lined up under my spirit, taking their orders.

"And here is my little finger, like my body, tucked in under my soul, feeling good 'cause I'm all integrated with Jesus, like Jesus is with God.

"Well, how did I do with the hand parable this time, Nan? I remember when you first drew that picture for me. You had to explain it a couple of times. Once I got it, I thought I would never forget it. But today I forgot it when I was so upset with Mom.

"It's so simple when things are the way God wants them to be. He wants our spirit to be in control of us, under the authority of His Holy Spirit, right? Nan, what if I forget again? What if I forget?"

"Lannie, we're going to pray right now," I said, diving into it. "Lord, sometimes we really need You to remind us about the way life in You is supposed to be. So by Your Holy Spirit please tug us at the elbow to restrain us (however You do that spiritually) when we forget our spirit is supposed to rest under Your Spirit's authority. Or put Your hand in the middle of our back, as it were, to give us a little push in the right direction when we need it. If that direction is what the Bible says, we know it's You.

"Thank You that when we are upset and confused, we can pray with our spiritual language and release our spirit to take its rightful place as guide, comforter and teacher....all those great biblical roles we can walk in as believers submitted to You. Then we can work in harmony with Your Holy Spirit. In Jesus' Name we pray this. Amen."

Lannie was praying loudly and joyfully in her spiritual language now. She stopped long enough to say, "My spirit, full of the joy of the Lord, is leading the way for my mind, will, emotions and body that are all marching in step right behind."

When Lannie hung up, she didn't say goodbye. She said, "Hallelujah!"

—❧—

I will pray with the Spirit, and I will also pray with the understanding... (1 Corinthians 14, 15).

Meanwhile, the moment we get tired in the waiting, God's Spirit is right alongside, helping us along. If we don't know how or what to pray, it doesn't matter. He does our praying in and for us, making prayer out of our

wordless sighs, our aching groans. He knows us far bet-
ter than we know ourselves. That's why we can be so sure
that every detail, in our lives of love for God, is worked
into something good (Romans 8:26-28 The Message).

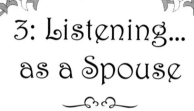

3: Listening... as a Spouse

In Her Eyes

what does a husband see when he looks into his wife's eyes

They were serious young wives who had each decided, despite considerable marital distress, to stay in her marriage and seek God's will for the life she should live with her husband.

Each woman was beginning to realize God's first clean-up project was herself, rather than husband or marriage. We met once a month to share, encourage, learn and pray together.

The doorbell would ring any minute. Gathering up my Bible and discussion notes, I felt there was something more I was supposed to share tonight. God knows how to get our attention. Making a brief mirror check, I patted a wisp of hair into place and found myself staring into the mirror, not quite sure why.

"What do you see?" said the Holy Spirit, matching my thoughts.

"My eyes looking back at me," I said tentatively.

"What does a husband see looking back at him when he looks into the eyes of his wife?" He prompted.

I thought about that. Sometimes a wife's eyes can communicate disapproval, disappointment, even frustration. I squirmed. A husband doesn't need that. He needs positive support from his wife. But if she feels negative about what's going on, shouldn't she be honest as well?

"Ask Me," said the Spirit, "and I'll say that she can be honest when things aren't right and still respond positively, lovingly."

"How can she respond positively to a bad situation?" I puzzled.

"Ask Me," the Spirit said again. "And I'll ask you if a husband looks into the eyes of the one closest to him, and can't find honesty and respect, truth and encouragement there, where will he look for them? When he's under stress, let him find those good things in her eyes, and in her hands let there be some little gift of practical loving-kindness to affirm what he sees in her eyes."

I settled into my armchair, thinking I'd ask the women when they arrived in a few minutes, what I was asking myself: What are little acts of kindness we each in our own households could do to show our husbands we appreciate and respect them, even when we don't totally agree with them in everything?

"Is that Your suggestion for me, Lord?" I smiled, picturing my husband about to head out to work a bit late, finding his polished shoes waiting for him at the front door. I liked it. It would work for Bill and me. Tucking a slip of paper into my Bible at Romans 8, I thanked the Lord for that insight about respect and practical loving-kindness and for this favorite Scripture to share with The Praying Wives.

There is therefore now no condemnation to those who are in Christ Jesus, who do not walk according to the flesh but according to the Spirit (Romans 8:1).

"Amen!" I said aloud, "that's so right. But then...it should be, shouldn't it? It's God's own Word!

"Fixed" In A Snowstorm

God at the end of my rope

You wouldn't find me out in a snowstorm with a light spring jacket over a tee-shirt and slacks. Not today. But some years ago, there was such a day.

On that day I was out there in a storm not caring that I was shaking with cold, that hot tears were melting snowflakes on my cheeks, that my feet were soaking wet.

I've long since forgiven and forgotten the domestic incident that drove me out into that storm. It also drove me to know God in a way I hadn't yet come to know Him. He, who was God at the end of my rope, gave me a blessing I've passed on to more than one troubled wife.

If I say I was escaping from an intolerable situation, that's not right: it was a situation I didn't want to tolerate. Abandoning any attempt to reason, I flung myself out the door, grabbed any jacket from the closet as I passed and instinctively slid a small Bible into its pocket.

A troubled soul can trudge only so far through a wet fall of snow before needing to talk. Who do you talk to in the middle of a snowstorm when most normal people are sitting together around the dinner table?

I took the little Bible from my pocket and standing under the lamp post, thumbed through its wet pages until I came to Psalm 108. The words flashed the strong, stable message I needed so badly: "O God, my heart is fixed! I will sing and give praise, even with my glory" (KJV).

It was the first time in my early Christian walk that the Holy Spirit had led me to a specific scripture. As I read it through snowflake-laden lashes, I knew it was for me. It was for me right now. And probably for me many times yet to come. (That would prove right!) At this point a scripture song from Psalm 34:1 kicked in from my memory at the gracious prompting of the Holy Spirit: "I will bless the Lord at ALL times, bless the Lord at ALL times, His praise shall continually be in my mouth!"

It didn't sound revolutionary, but it was exactly what I needed. I savored my two scriptures over and over again, returning them with gratitude to God, establishing them in my heart. I didn't yet grasp the significance they would have for the stability of my walk with the Lord in the years ahead, but they were speaking at that moment to my spirit. They were strengthening, calming and soothing my soul and they were giving me a critical perspective on my identity as one of His own.

As my reason gradually returned, I began to view my excursion into the snowstorm as some kind of adult tantrum; no help at all to the situation I'd been trying to escape. I wondered: if I hurried home, would my absence go unnoticed? Little hope of that since, by now, I looked like a drowned rat. When I began to giggle at my circumstances I knew my perspective was improving, that my spirit connected to God's Spirit, was in control. I couldn't excuse or condemn myself for my flight from my miserable situation but I could, and did, prepare myself to make apologies about a late dinner to the family.

Today, I love to stroll in the snow, enjoying the beauty of the scene and recalling the beauty of that night's revelation. My primary, privileged role is as His joyfully praising daughter and everything else falls into proper perspective as I honor that, no matter what "uglies" raise their heads.

A Hole In Our Spiritual Umbrella

the risk of an unrepaired tiff

What was the police cruiser doing in front of our house?

The upbeat mood of our church's New Year's Eve service vanished as we turned our car into our driveway.

A young officer stepped out of the cruiser and came to my window. "Ma'am, Sir, best leave the car here," he said as I lowered my window apprehensively.

"I'll be going into your house with you," he said, helping me out of the car. "The houses of your two next door neighbors have been broken into. We checked both houses out after they called to report.

"You're the last to get home. It's possible our cruiser lights have alerted the thieves. They may be hiding in your house."

As the officer accompanied me up the walk to the house, I was bewildered, "But we prayed protection over the house as usual before we left," I said to myself. But I had said it aloud.

"Oh really?" said the young policeman, putting his hand under my elbow as we climbed the steps to our front door. "Well, let's get in and see what's happened."

As I took the house key from my purse and slipped it into the lock, I thought, I think I'm about to learn something.

The policeman stepped in front of me to enter the house first. Our small cat, cringing in the recliner chair, clutched my arm as I picked her up. I gathered her little quaking body in my arms and stared at our disheveled living room. The officer slipped from room to room of our bungalow before heading for the basement. "No one up here," he whispered.

"I'll go down and check the basement. You take a look and see what's missing in the bedrooms, okay?"

The contents of my husband's file cabinet had been emptied and its contents strewn across the floor but everything seemed there.

I heard the policeman coming back up the stairs, calling out in a loud voice, "Nobody here either. But I can tell you how they got in. The same small individual who climbed through the cellar window off the driveway of both your neighbors' houses came through yours too. After he wriggles his way through a basement window he comes up to unlock the front door and let the others in. You should keep those windows locked.

"You going to be all right?" he said, putting a hand on my arm as I clutched my still cringing cat, "Doesn't look at first sight like they took too much, not like the other houses where they got TV's, money, jewelry and some rare liquor. Let's check about some more."

Closet doors had been opened and contents riffled. Dressers had been emptied and the desk dumped. But all we could find obviously missing was a bottle of loose coins worth about three dollars that had been on the kitchen window sill.

I laughed. My husband and the officer looked at me starkly: what was there to laugh about? Our home had been invaded! I saw their faces and laughed again as my nervous system unfroze. I stroked the cat and set her on the floor.

"I'm not sure I shouldn't feel insulted," I smiled in explanation. "Aren't our household effects worth stealing? But oh yes, I'm glad the little coin jar was all they took."

"They may not have had time to take anything more," the policeman pointed out. "I'd make a list of what they got, but you don't see anything else missing, I gather."

When we called our kids at their homes next morning to wish them Happy New Year, they reacted to our news with initial shock and then gratitude that the situation hadn't been more serious.

I expected some sort of professional assessment from my son, the correctional officer. But what I treasured was the assessment from my son, the Christian.

"The officer is right. Of course you should always keep the lock on windows when you're out, especially ground level windows. But you said you and Dad had an argument you didn't settle before leaving for church last night, eh? Hey, Momsy, you should always keep the lock on good relations too. The blood of Jesus covers believers but holding onto hard feelings punctures a hole in your umbrella!

"Sorry... enough with the sermon," he shook his head. "Somebody violated your privacy and you had a rude shock. But if the Lord hadn't been looking after you it could have been much worse, you know."

He was right. I've never forgotten the lesson God gave me via my son's comment. It went right into my tool repair kit... for whenever I have a tiff with a loved one.

Helpmate Waiting (For Women Only)

when a wife wants to be a help, not part of the problem

What is a woman's role...a godly woman's role...when she is not in spiritual step with her husband and everything she tries to do and be seems to worsen the situation and increase tension?

No thinking woman wants to pervert the role God has given her as a helpmate for her husband. She needs a revelation of the capacity she is to fulfill when her mate is under duress lest she interfere with God's timed plan for his life.

God once gave me a powerful image of this role that has resided in my spirit and blessed and nourished my soul to this day. It's been shared with many a troubled wife.

He showed me that above all, a wise woman keeps her spiritual armor in place. She keeps her footing in the Spirit. As she is shod with the preparation of the gospel of peace (Ephesians 6:15), no emotional carpet can be yanked out from under her, to draw her into reactions that make her appear the source of the problem. Such a devilish smoke screen would stop a man from seeing the real source of attack against him. A favorite device in Satan's "Marriage-mess" program is to try to disable the best prayer warrior a man could ever have: his wife!

This is the vision The Lord gave concerning the role of the prayer warrior wife:

Covered in a light-colored garment, a robe, a mantle, a cloak, the woman kneels, head bowed, still, but not passive.

Her action is in her prayer.

She is not aware of her visibility as pale gold Shekinah glory streams down upon and around her.

The color of her robe speaks of a righteousness, a gentleness, a purity, a deep God-consciousness.

It speaks of a distinct peace, an express wisdom, a special strength, a particular, specifically assigned ministry.

Eyes closed in focused intercession to God, she kneels facing the man who stands under this same light flooding over the situation.

She has a part in a God-work affecting her mate for the Lord has ordained that she take on this secret but essential work of prayer that will continue unhindered under His protection.

She is shielded from the turmoil surrounding her mate, while not removed from the situation.

The robe she wears is put on by faith.

It shapes specifically to her individuality as she receives it from God's hand and conforms to it.

She must put it on herself, willingly, anew, afresh every day, for without it, she has little protection and will become a distraction, part of the problem...or all of it, in the eyes of the man.

Without this garment-mantle-robe, she will become a stumbling block, a shade between the man and the work of God's Spirit flowing about him.

Abiding in His rest, His prayer-warrior daughter, wearing the prayer garments He has given, will be part of the Lord's answer for her husband.

God will speak to her in those secret moments with Him to receive essential wisdom to intercede for this man in keeping with God's will, way and Word.

Sense the expectancy, the knowing, the assurance that this is for a season until the time has come for these two to enter into the harmony of loving service together for their God.

Once readied by God, it will be the role of the man, to lift her from this place of consecrated prayer to stand by his side as his God-given helpmate that they may carry out God's purpose together, united in His Spirit, a powerful instrument in His hand.

Behold how good and how pleasant it is for Brethren to dwell together in unity. For there the Lord commands the blessing, life forevermore (from Psalm 133).

—⟨⟩⟨⟩—

"I-Forgive-You" Is An Action Word

a little act of kindness completes a change of heart

"Oh I forgive him, I forgive him all right. My record's clear. I've done that. I don't need to hear any more about it."

That's what my friend said. I wanted to believe her but there was such a hard edge to her voice, such a hard look on her face that I suspected her heart was just as hard. She'd been hurt and although she'd made the Christian response of speaking forgiveness to her husband, the hurt was obviously clinging like a leech.

I knew what her reaction would be if I suggested her underlying anger belied her forgiveness. Certainly, speaking forgiveness had been a start to the release of her hurt and anger. But there was more she needed to realize and I wanted to share that in a way she could receive it.

As I "studied how to answer" my friend (Proverbs 15:28), the Lord stirred in my memory, the picture of a time past when I had spent angry moments marching alone around my room, speaking forgiveness. It had been the last thing my aching heart wanted to do but it was right thing to do. God required it (Mark 11:25), so I did it.

No matter how difficult it was to do it, I regained my peace after I'd spoken forgiveness. About half an hour later, I remember that determined walk around my room, and asked myself, Now what was I going on so about?

"You knew God would give you the grace to forgive as you lined up your mouth with His Word," the Holy Spirit said and I nodded. I could smile at what now was a funny little memory of that feisty walk.

"But when did you feel the peace that comes with a forgiving heart?" the Holy Spirit prompted me. "And when did your love towards your husband resurface?"

"When I forgave him and turned the matter over to You," I said.

"And..." pressed the Holy Spirit.

"And... You asked me if I were willing to prove my forgiveness to him and to myself by doing something for him," I said remembering gratefully.

Now, here, in this moment with my friend, remembering those moments of my own when the Lord had given me His help to obey His Word and forgive, I wanted that same experience for her. I wanted to see the hurt in my friend's eyes replaced by the kind of joy that had filled me that day as I'd headed for the mending basket to sew a button back on my husband's favorite jacket.

God didn't ask me to move a mountain, but to do for my husband a little act of kindness, with a willing heart, in Jesus' Name.

I told my friend about the gentle lesson the Lord had taught me and the special sense of release I'd experienced as I had sewed on that little button.

Her frown quite vanished and her face opened up as the corners of her mouth turned up in a smile. I knew my point was being received.

"I'd say you're sharing your wealth!" she said, "and I'm accepting it!"

"Yes you can say that," I smiled back. "Life in Jesus, the way He asks us to live it, is rich."

The blessing of the Lord makes one rich and He adds no sorrow with it (Proverbs 10:22).

Yield To Wield

the sword of the Spirit comes with a price

Which is harder: going through a life storm or watching someone you care for go through it?

I used to think it was harder to go through a trial myself until I watched Annie stiffen her neck and make fists when I would have been bolting into my prayer room to ask God to show me what I was doing to make my husband so hostile.

It took a few heartbreaks before I learned to check out my own culpability as a first measure in dealing with marital upset. If God gave me a clean bill of spiritual health (it has happened on occasion!) I could look elsewhere for reasons behind our conflict so I could pray and behave appropriately.

Annie refused to entertain the idea that she might be part of her own problem. She was in no mood to listen, not to God, not to a good friend. So of course I told her anyway.

"Annie, if you can't break before God, you're going to get broken. If you can't take that mask of defiance off, you're going to fall flat on your face. God wants to deal with you tenderly but like a stubborn mule digging in your heels, you won't respond to 'tender'. God wants to shape a better you, but you keep pushing His hand away."

Well, that was blunt. Not my usual style really, but it seemed necessary. My resolve to be firm wavered a bit as I watched Annie's chin quiver. I knew she was hurting but sometimes the needle pricks when it plunges into a garment that needs repair.

My heart hurting with hers, we got on our knees in prayer to ask God's help.

No, Annie couldn't change her husband so that their marriage would be better. But she could ask God where she needed to change and grow and ask His help to do it. There was no way she could be effective for God if she couldn't yield to Him.

Annie admitted she could go it alone for just so long, looking for solutions, drumming up justification for herself whenever tempers flared and things got dicey. She agreed, maybe it was time to look at the situation for God's perspective.

I gave her one perspective, a bit of poetic prose that came out of a trial of my own years before. (Annie adopted it.)

When we spot our flaws,
when our rough edges cut others,
we yield to the Lord that His miracle working fingers
may mend torn flesh, strengthen weak wills,
transform distorted personalities,
repair shattered vessels
that submit to His peerless touch.
Then will we become mountain movers,
trail blazers, power conductors,
people picker-uppers, compassion administrators,
praise lifters, glory shiners,
for His loving purposes,
wielding the sword of His Spirit,
that is the Word of God.

Therefore as the elect of God, holy and beloved, put on tender mercies, kindness, humility, meekness, longsuffering; bearing with one another and forgiving one another, if anyone has a complaint against another; even as Christ forgave you, so you also must do (Colossians 3:12,13).

Doorknob Doctrine (For Men Only)

an alert coming in at the front door

Usually putting finishing touches on supper, this night I was ready early and sitting by the window as my husband came up the front steps from work.

When he didn't open the door and come in, I craned my neck to see him just standing there for several minutes.

"Got a surprise for me?" I smiled as he came in, waiting to see something come from his pocket that he'd secreted away there at the door.

"No... why?" he asked curiously.

I felt a little foolish explaining, but indeed, it was a gift for me that had taken his time at the front door.

"Ooohhh, I see," he chuckled. "Well, I use the doorknob as a checkpoint every night. The Lord got on my case a few months ago and I made a promise not to bring home any grumps or grumbles from the office. The doorknob is my reminder, my attitude checkpoint. If I've got stuff hanging on, it only takes a minute to wash with a bit of prayer.

"You like me clean?" he smiled as he got his welcome-home hug.

4: Listening... as a Parent

Hyper Baby, Hyper Mom

when parenting is intimidating

As a teenager, I was a conscientious, capable baby sitter.

As a married woman raising baby number one, the difference between baby sitting and baby parenting was intimidating. While still conscientious I was a distinctly hyper mom.

God changed that tense behavior with two life-changing events. The first was meeting Jesus when our baby wasn't quite two. With Jesus as my Savior and Lord, I came to view life in a new and wonderful way which included recognizing the parenting role as one of awesome privilege and responsibility. I tried not to let my Lord down, but often felt I fell short of the mark. The second life-changing event was four years later when Jesus baptized me in His Holy Spirit. I began to see life through His eyes as never before. One of the first things I saw was that my hyper attitude had created a hyper child.

Without condemning me, the Lord let me grieve until I accepted His empowerment to live and model His peace and to mother my child with quiet effectiveness. Night after night while she slept, God drew me back to her bedside to lay hands on her in Jesus' Name, claiming His peace and rest.

Those were precious, heart-tugging hours by the bedside of this dear little person.

Today our daughter is a competent, caring, effective social work executive. One of her strongest characteristics is His abiding peace.

—❧❧—

Spider!

the Lord cuts a phobia from our generational line

Yes, I screamed every time I saw a spider. I told myself lots of women scream when they see a mouse. I said it was the same thing but it wasn't. Spiders had power over me.

Since childhood, I'd felt a chill run down the side of my face at the sight of a spider. I accepted that fear as something to endure.

My children's response to my "spider nerves" made me question my acceptance of that fear. As they left infancy, I became concerned about their vociferous reaction to the eight-legged little beasties. It didn't take a detective to see who my children's role model was. Little kids soak up environment and spider phobia was part of the world I was building around them. Something had to change.

It had been time for a change for some time but I hadn't been able to see it despite having learned as a young Christian that fear isn't part of anyone's heritage in Christ Jesus. Revelation and motivation were needed because I'd become accommodated to this phobia.

My kids had become my motivation and now revelation was on its way as the Holy Spirit brought to my remembrance my little basement playhouse of early childhood. Here I would happily make tea from any berry-type of bush in our garden. My big sister was my best guest as she'd enthuse over every cup she raised to her lips without, fortunately, ever swallowing a drop. This day I was eagerly waiting for my best guest to come to my tea party, humming a little tune to hurry the waiting.

Suddenly I was screaming. The sound of my terror ascended the stairs, bringing everyone in the house. Shaking all over, eyes wide with shock, I fell into Mother's arms and sobbed. The instant of terror, as a spider had trailed down the side of my face, was etched into my nervous system.

It stayed etched from that day until God's intervention answered my desire to be free of this inane spider fixation for my children's sake. Seeing the root of the phobia, I didn't enjoy the recollection and, rather like a child limping to my daddy's knee with a scraped elbow, I pouted and presented my scarred memory to God.

"I was there to hold and heal you then, even before you knew Me," He said gently. "But now you know Me and now you can accept your healing after these many years. There is no time with Me."

Oh yes, I thought, delighting in His gracious healing of my "spider memory" in that moment, Jesus is the same, yesterday and forever – Hebrews 13:8.

Then, from somewhere inside my spirit, a little chuckle followed the revelation and assurance: maybe I should forgive the spider! Another chuckle surfaced as I imagined the distress my scream must have caused the poor icky little thing.

Maybe I'll just ask Spider to forgive me for shocking him out of his tiny, little spider wits! I smiled to myself.

I imagined Spider, doing his spider thing, looking for a good spot to set up housekeeping, descending to our basement floor on his slender strand of silk, carefully threading his way on all eight little legs down this convenient post (me!) under the lintel of my playroom door. My screech, right under his little spider nose must have split the air and made every hair on his fuzzy little body stand on end.

Because I've always loved the creatures God has made (except for spiders up to that point), I now delighted to find humor, tolerance, even compassion working in my heart for another one of His amazingly created little critters. My next chuckle was in remembering that joy is a sign of a healed memory.

As with all memories healed by the Holy Spirit, my childhood spider story can no longer distress me. But it is part of my store of experiences with the Lord that I can call on to help others, anytime any of those experiences are appropriate. A great thing about a healed memory is that what Satan intends for ill, God can use for good, as Joseph declares triumphantly in Genesis 50:20.

Postscript: The next time we found a spider in the house, my kids were properly impressed as I calmly took its silken thread between my thumb and finger to escort it outside. I remember saying something like, "Sorry, fella...wrong place, wrong time."

They never did master the technique of silk thread transport, but they did learn to scoop up spiders with tissue and pop them outside without squishing them!

God is faithful and His sense of humor endures forever. Just think how arachnophobia halted its progress down the generational line that day the Lord tickled my funny bone.

Balancing Gripes With Blessings

though children are trying at times...

I was grumbling, but trying not to sound like it, even to myself. "I do love having the children's friends here. And it means I can know where my own kids are and that everything is all right because I'm right here to see it is."

"But..." prompted the Holy Spirit.

"But...well...," I said, trying to sort out why I was feeling so irritated.

Recognizing that I was so irritated was a start. And with that recognition, I found myself remembering the sight of little Andy from down the street, walking down my hallway after playing in my back yard, trailing his fingers along my wall on either side as he made his way to my bathroom.

"But...much as I love having the kids here, I think I don't love scrubbing these grubby little fingermarks off the wall every time they leave!"

"Which would you rather have," asked the Holy Spirit gently, "the grubby little fingermarks or the little fingers that made them?"

"Oh," I smiled, "that's easy! The little fingers of course!"

A pause, as the thought sifted down, "The grubby little finger marks come with the little fingers."

Another lesson for life from the Maker of little fingers, I laughed and went back to scrubbing the wall.

—⟨⟩⟨⟩—

Hope Out Of Sadness For A Little One

seizing life's opportunities to tell God's stories

The chuckle rising in my throat died as I sensed a check in my spirit from the Lord. "This is not just a cute scene. Her sorrow is real. It's your opportunity to teach your daughter a life lesson."

When my five-year-old had set out for kindergarten that fall morning, frost had touched the flowers that we had enjoyed and picked for the table all summer long. Lovingly sensitive to every living thing, here she was, coming back into the house sobbing, her arms full of wilting blossoms.

To this mother's eye it did look cute and a little joke about Jack Frost getting in his licks early this year seemed appropriate until the Holy Spirit quickened my discernment. I took the languishing flowers from her, laid them gently on the table and drew her onto my lap.

I was able to present to her God's wonderful story of the seasons, death and new life to come, on a level she could grasp, asking the Holy Spirit all the while to express these beautiful Christian truths through me to her open child's heart and mind.

She had never before taken note of autumn's icy hand, but God knew my little daughter was ready that morning for her first lesson of Life over death.

—ᢙᢙ—

The Holy Spirit Referees A Fight

little people learn from little events

It's a good thing the Holy Spirit understands kids! I was looking for all the help I could get when our little visitor stood before me, her blond curls shaking almost imperceptibly despite her attempt at a nonchalant pose.

I drew her to me and asked her help in discovering how her two playmates had bloodied their noses. Everything about her said she knew more than she was letting on. I was armed with one fact at least. I had heard her voice under my kitchen window urging, "Hit him. He was mean to me. You gotta hit him."

"You gotta hit him," she had said. Her parents taught her not to fight but revenge was in her heart, desire for it was in her voice. One of her playmates had charged to her defense just that much faster than the time it had taken my feet to get on site after hearing those words.

Mending relations here would need an honest view of the goings-on. Her body language tallied with what I'd heard through the window, but I needed more to work with, than the fact that she'd instigated a fight. The moment would be too far removed for anything constructive to come out of this if we waited for her mom to come home and deal with it.

Was this really a small matter; just a tempest in a teapot? Was I trying to make too much of a little incident? I believe such small incidents are big matters to little people who learn from happenings that may seem insignificant to adults. I welcomed this event as an opportunity to help the children gain some understanding and skill for conflicts that can spring up in relationships at any time.

The three strategic words, "Immediate, Fair and Consistent" from my Child Psychology II course years ago, rang as loud in my memory as when our professor had pounded it into his students. He'd taught us godly principles of child rearing from the Old Testament...and this at a time before I'd met Jesus, "the Word made flesh" (John 1:15).

I admit that since she'd chosen my son as her champion, I was not too pleased with little blondie, but I didn't want to embarrass her before these two already provoked little boys. So I entered the situation to mediate with my Psych II training and the few facts I could see.

"But aren't you missing something?" whispered the Holy Spirit. "She may have been taught not to fight but she doesn't know why not to fight and has absolutely no idea how to handle conflict."

With that thought in mind, I was able to ease the tension with a smile and a shake of my head, a bit of soap, a wet rag, band-aids and chocolate milk. I put my arms around the three little people for some gentle but firm "plain talk". It included gently applying verses to our situation from a children's version of the Bible using Luke 1:79, John 14:27, Romans 2:10 and 1 Corinthians 14:33. They seemed to receive it and I trusted that they would understand a little more of their life in Jesus and how it works.

Now, the "mean" little boy was not yet a believer, so this was an introduction for him to a "whole 'nother way of life", as my kids would say. A few months later the family moved to another city. But knowing a seed has to be planted before it sprouts, we included in our bedtime prayers that night, a blessing upon the little seed we'd planted that day, to take root and grow in his life.

Pillow Talk

understanding a teenager: going where she is

"Pillow Talk" was always special when our kids were young. This was a time to sit in the intimate half-light at bedtime to ask how things were, really were, if signs of reticence or sadness had been detected that day.

We would gather any untied threads of the day, listen in empathy and pray these things into the Lord's hands. Their confessions, hopes, ideas and fears were expressed as at no other time. Trust was built deeply into our relationship with our children that would stand us in good stead for the years to come.

A few years later, I discovered another kind of "pillow talk" that would allow me to relate to our daughter as she entered her teen years. A distance sprang up between us that seemed unbridgeable. In that first so-different high school year, our lovely, vibrant girl suddenly became uncommunicative.

The emptiness of our farewell at the door one morning as she went off to class chilled my heart. I went to her room and sank back against a puff of pillows arranged on her bed against the wall.

"Dear Lord," I prayed, "let me see what is dragging my girl down."

I stayed there a long while, hugging her pillows to myself. The Lord let me sense the bewilderment and insecurity that so often comes with that age as the sudden thrust into a world sets a different pace and whistles a different tune from the familiar ones of a Christian home.

Remembering my own early teen years, feelings of frustration about our relationship slipped away as I felt for her, wept for her and immersed myself in heartfelt intercession for her.

Some hours later, I met my cool one at the door, and where sympathy over her awkward feelings would have been unwelcome, her bridge began to lower before God's gift to me of empathy and quiet understanding.

Jesus has bridged the gap between men and God. He gives us grace to bridge the generation gap and willingness to walk a mile in our children's shoes that we might keep them company and join hands with them as we hear their concerns and joys.

The scene today is not as it was when we were children. But the wiles of Satan, the spirit of the world and the flesh itself are no different than they ever were.

To answer that threat, Jesus claps the spiritual weapons of wisdom, empathy, demonstrated love and intercession into the hands of parents who choose to listen to His Spirit for their battle orders.

"Gossamer Threads"

apron strings are sometimes hard to see

When my kids were in their mid-teens, the Lord used the image of "gossamer threads" to free them from "Parental Clutch" as they grew closer to a newer, adult relationship with Him.

"Parental Clutch?" How could that describe my loving parental mindset as my kids stretched (and sometimes tripped) towards adult independence? I was about to find out as Christmas festivities came to a close that year.

When I brought to God vague, uneasy feelings about my changing relationship with my maturing kids, much to my surprise He gave me a clear picture of allegorical apron strings I had recently severed from both son and daughter. He showed the apron strings obviously still in place and tied quite securely.

But I had severed those apron strings months ago when the Holy Spirit had shown how I was unwittingly hobbling my children to myself instead of helping them grow as individuals with their God. Well, the Holy Spirit was alerting me that I was doing it again. I'd fallen into a "flesh" rut once more, binding them to myself in selfish concern for their welfare in the big challenging world they were stepping into. I knew dependence on God was the prime relationship they needed now, and for the rest of their lives.

Once more I surrendered my kids to God, taking my hands off, while staying alert with godly concern and parental caring that will continue as long as I'm their Mom.

A few days later, at the New Year's Eve service, our pastor spoke of dealing before God with things that could hinder our walk with Him in the coming year. We were asked to make a heart attitude check. I was confident I'd done what we were being admonished to do since I'd just been through this with the Lord already, divesting myself and my children of those maternal apron strings. But who can afford to take the Holy Spirit for granted? I did a recheck of my heart file labeled, "Loved Ones, Outstanding Matters". Just as I thought, I told myself, nothing there. I sat back, certain everything was covered.

Then I heard that still small voice (1 Kings 19:12). "Look again."

"Lord?" I questioned as I saw with the eye of my spirit what looked like slender filaments threading from my fingertips to both my son and daughter.

"Barely discernible, but definitely there again are those soul ties," said the Holy Spirit matter-of-factly. "Slender, gossamer threads, that seem of little significance now, can become as restrictive as hemp rope or chain mail unless you release your children from your own emotional reactions. You have been a careful, caring mother to the best of your ability. They are entering young adulthood now. Release them again. This time release them for all time, into My hands to guide, protect and equip them for the life I have prepared for them.

"Take the sword of the Spirit, the Word of God, and cut those gossamer threads of flesh. Whom the Son sets free is free indeed (John 8:36). Let their lives be directed by My touch. I call you to the role of a prayer warrior on their behalf.

"And more than this, embrace the habit of soon and often submitting every relationship you have to Me. You are never closer to your loved ones than when My Spirit dwells between you. Soul ties, even gossamer ones, show little trust in your loved ones and little faith in Me to shepherd them."

Strong words from our powerful God. If I trusted God's firm, gracious shepherding of my own life, how could I not trust my maturing children to His care? That gentle rap on my spiritual knuckles was effective. "Watch for gossamer threads," He had said. "There's no place for those in your relationship with these children growing into adulthood."

Once when I was taking a quick check for those threads, He gave me this lovely reassurance, "One day they will be two of your best friends, grateful with you for the generous care of the loving God you share."

About Parental Mistakes

how the kids think about them

After a few spiritually scraped knees as a parent, I'd learned and was determined to never second-guess the Lord if He asked me to do something that looked difficult.

So I was ready that Christmas Day. As I prepared to maneuver a 20-pound turkey from pan to platter, the Holy Spirit dropped a strong directive among my thoughts.

"Now, ask him now."

The "him" was my son Larry, sitting with his pregnant wife in the relative peace of our living room. The rest of the family was setting out Christmas presents in the family room downstairs and I was putting the finishing touches on Christmas dinner.

The "ask" was something the Lord had said I should do while I'd been wrapping a gift for this first grandchild who would soon be making his appearance into this world. Watching my son over the past few months adjust to his new role as father-to-be, I had wondered about times I'd missed the still small voice of God (1 Kings 19:12) during his growing-up years. How might my mistakes affect my son's own parenting?

"What do You say about that, Lord?" I had asked as I had tied the bow on First Grandchild's present.

"Ask Larry," had come the simple reply.

Now, heading slowly for the living room, I smoothed my Christmas apron and thought again just how I'd ask.

"Larry," I said, moving right into it, "it was always my intention to bring you up as God would have me do, but sometimes I wasn't listening and I made mistakes. The thing is that you'll have to work out with God, the effects in your life of the mistakes I made in your upbringing. Can you forgive me for any poor parenting I've done?"

There was a lot of quiet after that as Larry looked at his socks, so I went back to my steaming turkey. But before I could get a handle on the beast, from the living room came a summons. "Mom. Come. Take off your apron. Sit."

Well, I thought as I complied, I asked for it.

"In the first place," he said, reaching forward to pat my hand, a smile lurking around his eyes, "I did think at times that my Mom wasn't always fair. Most of the time I really knew you were and was actually glad when you were tough with me. Believe it or not. I'm thinking now that there must have been times when you should have been tougher, no matter what I thought then. Point is...you were there and you cared. And it came across big. Thanks, Mom," he finished his speech, crowning it with a big bear hug.

I returned to the turkey, hoping no one would find it a mite too salty if it was now laced with a few grateful tears as I swung it onto the platter.

Yes, it's true that parents are accountable to God for parental management. It's also true that kids are not made of eggshell. And it's true that they know when our love is real and when we earnestly try to follow after the only perfect parent, God. I believe when that is so, they do forgive our blunders... especially when they begin to make their own mistakes with their own kids.

God Holds The Other End
Of A Daughter's Rope

...and recruits a mom intercessor

My friend Laurie was smiling through her tears. As I listened, I didn't see much to smile about. Her daughter's life had taken a bad turn. The young woman was a Christian but it seemed the situation she was in at the moment, was not.

Laurie was stunned when she discovered the situation her girl was in. "She didn't grow up in a Christian home learning the values she's living by now," she said. "We seemed to be in separate worlds. I didn't know how to reach my child."

Laurie never hesitated to go into her prayer room when life was confusing or difficult. This time, she ran.

"I got on my knees and pulled on that prayer line like I've never pulled on it before!" she said, gripping my hand as she recalled those difficult hours searching for answers.

"I gave the Lord the whole situation as I'd discovered it and spewed out my hurt, disappointment, anger and fear for my darling girl. Lying on my bed, exhausted, I cried, 'Lord, I don't even know how to talk to her. I don't know where her heart is. I don't know where she's going. I only know she's heading for disaster. What's going to happen to my baby?'"

Laurie described a hush, a peace that filled the room, bringing with it a quiet expectation. In that moment, she sensed she was about to hear something from God that would bring hope, even point out the direction she should follow to help her child.

"I must tell you about the rope," Laurie told me, eyes wide with remembered excitement as she launched into a description of the picture with which God's Holy Spirit answered her cry in that quiet moment. Whether it was a dream, or a vision, Laurie found comfort and assurance as she "saw" in the spirit what was to happen to the young woman she had raised to love the Lord and delight in His will.

Laurie had seen a long rope hanging from somewhere, tailing off somewhere else. She couldn't see the bottom end of it but she did see a great hand holding the rope from above. But whose hand was it? And where did the rope go? What was it being used for?

"The hand is Mine," answered the Lord, dropping His thoughts among her thoughts. "Our Angela is on the other end of this rope. I'll not let go of that rope unless she chooses to cut loose from My grasp. When you brought her to Me as a child, she asked Me into her life. As I have given each of My children free will, she may choose her own life direction even if that direction pains both you and Me.

"I've let this rope pay out as she has exercised that free will, even if that free will has carried her into the situation that binds her now. But you must know this: that rope is secure about her. That rope is My Holy Spirit's presence within her, reminding her that she is My beloved child. One day she will come to the end of her rope. One day in her desperation, she will cry out to her Lord, known and loved all the years of her youth. I wait for that cry. And I will use your faith as you pray in the name of My Son for that day to come quickly."

As she let these thoughts anchor in her heart, God's Spirit gave Laurie another picture in her mind's eye of her daughter at the end of that rope, twisting and turning as her deviant lifestyle pulled her down into pain and sorrow. Her face contorted with fear, Angela turned her eyes upward to frantically cry out, "Lord! Please forgive me and help me get out of here" (Psalm 123: 1, 2).

"Free will is hers to choose even wrong paths," the Holy Spirit spoke into Laurie's thoughts, "but the love of God will pursue her to persuade her with conviction, never condemnation. Your girl chose that evil lifestyle, but as she refuses its control in Jesus' Name, the Lord will make use of all this for His own purposes. When your Angela calls, God will hear and will redeem."

Laurie held her breath as she "watched" God draw up the rope, hand-over-hand until the young woman swung high above the situation that threatened to reap her soul.

Laurie's face was radiant as she told how she "saw" Angela, once more in the hands of her Lord, fall to her knees in repentance and joy. Angela was home, safe once more, determined as never before to stay under the shadow of His wings (Psalm 17:8).

Laurie's laughter rose as she pumped my hand up and down with excitement, "You should have seen the way the Lord let that rope pay out as Angela went her own way. Then when she cried out to Him, dangling at the end of her rope, how tenderly and firmly He drew her back to Himself. He has told me to pray, binding the evil spirit behind that lifestyle until the wooing of His Holy Spirit turns her heart. God will hear. He will redeem. He will bring her home.

"And then," Laurie said, clapping her hands together in eager anticipation, "I can pray for opportunities she'll have to share about her rescue from that awful life. God didn't cause her fall but He will use her story to share with others who need to hear how God's love persists."

At this point, Laurie and I were brimming over with praise and thanksgiving for what God had promised and what He was about to do. She reached for her concordance and drew her finger down the pages of Psalms, looking for those that praise the Lord for His hand on the lives of those who call upon Him.

The words seem to spring off the page as we called out our "amens" after so many of them. Here are a few:

Let Your hand become my help, for I have chosen Your precepts (Psalm 119:173).

That Your beloved may be delivered, save me with Your right hand and hear me (Psalm 60:5).

Though I walk in the midst of trouble, You will revive me: You will stretch out Your hand against the wrath of my enemies and Your right hand will save me (Psalm 138: 7).

Where can I go from Your Spirit? Or where can I flee from Your presence? If I ascend into heaven, You are there. If I make my bed in hell, behold You are there. If I take the wings of the morning and dwell in the uttermost parts of the sea, even there Your hand shall lead me. And Your right hand shall hold me (Psalm 139: 7-10).

Stretch out Your hand from above. Rescue me and deliver me out of great waters, from the hand of foreigners, whose mouth speaks lying words and whose right hand is a hand of falsehood. I will sing a new song to You, O God, on a harp of ten strings, I will sing praises to You (Psalm 144:7).

You have also given me the shield of Your salvation: Your right hand has held me up (Psalm 18:35).

The right hand of the Lord is exalted, the right hand of the Lord does valiantly, I shall not die but live, and declare the works of the Lord (Psalm 118:16).

Oh, sing to the Lord a new song! For He has done marvelous things: His right hand and His Holy arm have gained Him the victory (Psalm 98:1).

Laurie looked at me. "And we know who God's Right Hand is!" She took her Bible and turned to Hebrews 2:1, 2:

...let us lay aside every weight, and the sin which so easily ensnares us, and let us run with endurance the race that is set before us, looking unto Jesus, the author and finisher of our faith, who for the joy that was set before Him, endured the cross, despising the shame and has sat down at the right hand of the throne of God (Hebrews 12:1,2).

I was overjoyed for what was in store for my friend and her daughter even though I never did know the details of the situation. Angela would, and did, escape. But this story isn't so much about what Angela went through. It's about God impressing on a frantic parent His faithfulness to rescue a lost child. It's about the mandate He has given us to intercede for our children all the days of our lives.

_____ Ꮼ Ꮼ _____

Daughter Space, Mother Space

as two adults now, we meet for lunch

I'd forgotten a prime directive I had learned from the Lord, about gracefully relating to a grown daughter as friend first, mother second.

My daughter, as executive director of a vibrant social work agency, is problem-and-solution oriented, practical, wise, decisive and innovative. Her mother, as an author and freelance journalist, observes, questions, researches, defines, chronicles. Both investigative, both analytical, we still occupy different spaces.

Early for a lunch date with my daughter, I waited in her new seventh floor office at a wall-sized window looking out over a lush green landscape as she finished meeting with a staff member. Changes had taken place with this growing agency as its vital services became more and more visible in the community. This change of location was one, and my reporter's brain began considering the effect of it on the organization's image.

If she was looking forward to visiting with the friend-mother I've become, she certainly wasn't expecting the barrage of questions that met her as she entered her office to take me to lunch. I was definitely in my curious-journalist mode which is alright at the right time and place. This wasn't it.

In the elevator, she looked at me, "You nervous or something Dear? You're full of observations and questions...I don't mean to offend, Mom, but it's getting to me."

The "Mom" did it. I stepped back into my Mom-friend identity. I had given her a bizarre greeting with my barrage of questions that would have been hard enough to take from a friend, let alone a mom. Bizarre is ridiculous and can be laughable if you back up for a second look.

"Not nervous, just thoughtless." I smiled at her. "We're from different professional spaces. I just crashed yours. I observe and query to explore. You observe and query to direct. I've explored. You've directed. We've both done what we do best...professionally. And now we're going to lunch, so we can just be daughter and mom and have a good chin-wagging lunch."

Her amused but sedate grin said all was well and we went off to a fine lunch full of talk about mundanely delightful details and a few individual problems to discuss that friends, even mom-friends, can share.

"Lord," I whispered as I drove home after the lunch, "if I have to relearn any of the lessons You've taught me, may the learning always be this gentle."

5: Listening...
as a Grandparent

When A Prayer Seems To Miss The Mark

God provides better than we lose

I pray when I lose something and rejoice when I find it. But what about the times when something is not recovered after going to the Lord in prayer? Do we still recognize God as our loving provider?

A green garbage bag full of kids' clothes took care of that question for my two small grandchildren about to attend a new school in a new community.

I had noticed the bag of the boys' garments sitting at the curb ready to be loaded into their car that moving day. In speechless shock I watched the garbage man swing it into the truck just seconds later before I could shriek, "Stop!"

It was garbage collection day and the mistaken identity of the stuffed bag was understandable. But our two little fellas watching the truck move down the street with its loader grinding away were imagining a very blue first day at school without the clothes now being mashed to land fill.

To believe that God was going to bring a happy ending to this misfortune was a challenge for these little guys. But I prayed in faith in Jesus' Name. As the boys joined me in a heartfelt, "Amen," the Kid's Clothing Exchange in our church basement came to mind.

We headed for the church and by suppertime, every lost item was replaced from the church exchange. A "neat" array of toys that had been added as a bonus, helped wreathe the small faces in smiles, lift their spirits and confirm to us all, that God can provide better than we lose!

The Day Nana Lost Her Purse In The Park

little boys see Nana pray for guidance...and get it

It all began one beautiful, sunny spring day that the grandchicks were spending with me. We packed food and, leaving the car at home, set out for the local park by bus. At ages three and five, they were enamored of the big red and white vehicle, they affectionately called, "Big Red".

Little fellows that age aren't much help when it comes to toting a bag lunch for three, snacks for three, a picnic blanket, a diaper bag and Purse. I managed to get the stuff, the boys and myself on and then off "Big Red" all in one piece.

We found a lovely park site where we could see a stream, birds, kids coming from school at lunchtime and a setter with its nose to the ground, tracking a squirrel.

Peanut butter and jam sandwiches downed, we set out to see what adventure awaited us over the next hill. I loaded lunch remains, snack bag, picnic blanket and diaper bag. Then I struck out with the boys, grasping two little hands while balancing our load.

Several hills, a few float-the-twig-under-the-bridge races, a visit with the setter and three weed bouquets later, we decided a ride home on "Big Red" would be welcome. I fixed the boys still with my eye as I shifted bags and blanket to fish the bus fare from Purse.

Purse wasn't there.

Initial reaction to hightail it back to the picnic site where Purse was last seen, soon gave way to reality at the sight of two tired little faces. I couldn't carry two husky boys back to the picnic spot nor leave them behind while I retraced my steps to our picnic spot.

We sat down so Nana could collect her thoughts. Purse was quite lost and with Purse, the fare back home. Home was only fifteen minutes away by bus. I woefully estimated the time it would take to walk the distance. Moving at their weary pace would we make home by bedtime? Hitchhiking would be a last resort, but we were running out of options.

I held little hands in mine, looked up through the canopy of trees to the clear sky and spoke to the One who knew our plight. "Lord, we can't see any good way to get home. What should we do? I'm so sorry I was careless about Purse. We trust You and thank You that you will show us how to get back home."

We started out, singing little songs to encourage expectations. Leaving the park, crossing to the bus stop, we passed a gate beyond which we could hear conversation and a couple of quietly whirring little machines that piqued our curiosity. The machines had moved away by the time we got there but another two came up behind us and stopped. Golfers sitting in the machines stared at us. We had wandered onto private golf club grounds.

"What are you doing here!" the first woman spoke loudly. "Do you realize you could be struck by a flying golf ball? You must get these children out of here at once."

The grandchildren had never seen Nana babble before, but finally, with lame gestures, I told the story of our predicament.

The lady golfer's face softened and she said, "I'm a grandmother too. You must get the boys home after all this excitement. Here's money for the bus. Hope you get your purse back."

When their parents arrived to pick them up after supper, the boys threw themselves upon them to tell the tale in stereo, excitedly sharing the details of "How God got us home when Nana lost Purse."

Purse was delivered the next day by a generous dog walker from the park who had found our address inside, brought it to our door and was now apologizing for not being able to return it as soon as he'd found it.

The boys listened with interest to our benefactor, especially when he tipped his hat and left, calling back, "God bless you!" to which First Grandson leaned out the door and replied brightly, "He did, mister. He already did!"

What Did He Say? What Did He Say?

little boys agree with the Lord's wisdom

Grandad was testy. Grandad was grumpy. In fact, he was downright hedge-hoggy.

In the middle of our discussion about where to go for supper to end this nice afternoon drive with our two visiting grandsons, a car suddenly cut in front of us. Grandad raised his voice, slammed the car horn and thumped the driver's wheel. I looked around to the back seat to see two little pairs of widening eyes looking at the back of the driver's head: Could this be Papa?

At the breakfast table, the next morning, First Grandson slid into his seat, quiet again, something obviously on his eight-year-old mind.

"Nana, 'member Papa getting cross in the car yesterday?"

"Yes, when the driver from the next lane cut us off."

"Did you pray about it?"

"Yes," I said. "I asked God why Papa was so upset. He doesn't usually get so cross at someone doing something dumb like that driver was doing."

First Grandson looked up intently. "What did He say? What did He say?"

"Well," I said, "God reminded me of the pressure Papa's been under at work lately and I thought, God's reminding us about that so we'll be sure to be especially kind to Papa these days."

"That's a good answer!" he said, his face lighting up, "and we'll be sure to do that, right?"

It was and we did. It's not just the little people who learn about God's ongoing concern for us through everyday happenings. The big people do too.

—☙☙

6: Listening... as a Caregiver of an Aging Parent

Walking Her Beloved Hills

helping an aging parent adjust to new surroundings

Some fifty years ago, Mom and Dad built their home into the side of a hill that sloped to a meandering stream centering three acres. Widow and widower, they met and married in middle age. This lush wooded land was a continuing honeymoon site and they transformed it into a natural park with skill born of experience and loving care.

Dad died at ninety-two, looking out at his hills with his "bride" at his bedside. Mom found much comfort as we prayed. She knew God had supplied the strength and grace to give Dad this last gift of being able to end this life in the place they had both loved so much.

For five years Mom managed on her own. She tended the acreage, diligently keeping birds and blooms a happy part of that beautiful spot. My husband and I were proud of her, but knew, as she entered her ninety-first year, that it was time for her to leave her fort and come to live with us.

Knowing the role the acreage had played in her life for those four decades, I sensed some of the loss she must have felt as she surveyed her dear hills during those last months before moving across the province to live with us.

"Walked my beloved hills this morning," read her letters so often. And then one day, "Wanted to get out on my beloved hills today, but it was slippery. Didn't seem wise."

Those hills spoke to her of love when life was full and when it was laced with sorrow and loneliness. If I could have packed up her hills with her furniture, I would have done it. Then, quite simply, I found a wonderful thought hanging in my mind, like a memo on a peg from our loving Lord.

Mom came as summer was fading, still in time to walk the restored nature trail I had cut through the woods that surround the cul-de-sac where our home was located. It took me nine hours to trim. My husband made the generous claim that if taken slowly, the tour could be covered in almost five minutes.

Here Mom and I moved, from her hills to our trail, a dainty little Austrian pine, a bath of lily-of-the-valley, ginger plant, wild violet and jack-in-the-pulpit. We'd walk these little hills and valleys, kick through fallen leaves, look into waving branches above to squirrels scrambling in the trees, sit on stumps in the little ravine and smile at one another, remembering her beloved hills.

When we'd return to the house, Mother often sat at her organ and I'd hear again the precious strains, "I walked today where Jesus walked...my heart felt unafraid...." *

Thank You, Lord that You never leave us or forsake us and that Your word and Your creation constantly remind us of Your faithful loving kindness (Hebrews 13:5).

"I Walked Today Where Jesus Walked", copyright 1937, Jeoffrey O'Hara

Lost And Found

a God-incident brings joy out of loss

Across the miles, Mother's voice over the phone was staccato with worry, "Did you take my keys by mistake when you left?"

Pockets were checked, car was searched, purse upended and dumped. There was no sign of her keys.

This was not good. Living by herself since Dad had died, my aging mom was still not ready to abandon her three-acre home on the outskirts of a city two hours from us. Since making a job-related move, we had honored her desire for independence but had visited her weekly and relied on the phone for daily contact to make sure she was all right. Lost keys were a serious problem for an elderly woman on her own, living some distance from her closest neighbor.

As I looked to the Lord for help for her, I realized Mom could be doing the same. I called her back to say, "Have you prayed yet, Mom?"

"Oh no, what's the matter with me, I didn't pray!" she said.

"Let's!" I said and leapt into prayer. "God, You know where Mom's keys are. Please show her. Thank You, in Jesus' Name."

"Amen!" she exclaimed, excited in a different way now. "Call you as soon as I have them."

Ten minutes later the call came. "You'll never believe this. Yes, you will. I went to the closet right after we prayed and felt to look in the shoe bag. The keys were sitting right there. I must have dropped them there last night."

And then, "Thank You, Lord, I'd never have thought to look there."

God loves doing things like that for hearts that look to Him for answers, no matter how big or how small the problem is.

Fear Of Unknown
No Match For True Christmas Hospitality

God helps an elder change a lifetime prejudice

Ade was spending another Christmas far from his home in Nigeria.

Enthusiastic, open-minded, eager to experience Canadian culture while attending university here, he didn't expect the impact that our Canadian snow and ice would have on him. Nor did he have any idea of the impact that his presence would have on an older woman for whom the thought of entertaining a black man poured the ice of fear into her heart.

My husband, our two kids and I responded to an invitation from FROS (Friendly Relations with Overseas Students) which encouraged us to "take in a student from overseas who will otherwise be alone and lonely on campus while everybody else is home celebrating Christmas".

Our student was a sociable young man with a wide smile and hearty laugh. He was a story-teller who loved to sit by the fireside on those cold, winter nights and regale us with his stories.

Of all his stories, the one we all remember years later is Ade's first experience with snow. He attended a boys' college in England before coming to Canada. Studying in his dorm room one November afternoon, he saw "white feathers" dancing outside his window. Running to his roommate, he grabbed the book from his hand, pulled him to the window and pointed, speechless.

"Hey, Ade! Guess this is your first snow!" chuckled his friend. "Come on, let's get out there. It's time you got introduced to snow!"

Ade rushed out onto the amazing campus landscape, changing before his eyes into a big, white fairyland. He ran, laughed and danced in circles as falling snow swirled about him.

Suddenly he noticed he was cold and wet: very cold and very wet. He looked down at his soaked slippers, pulled his housecoat around him and shivered. Looking back, he saw how far he had sprinted from the dormitory. Through the thickening snow, he could barely see his roommate, standing in the dormitory doorway with his arms crossed and a big smile on his face.

"Ade," called his roomie, "you have to dress proper for that kind of running about! At least let's get some boots on you, lad!"

Ade looked almost sheepish as he waited to hear our response to the story of his first snowfall, but it was obvious he had enjoyed rehearsing every minute of it. He told us how he had prepared to come to Canada on scholarship, determined to earn top grades at university and make his parents proud. He also thought that because of his experience in England, he'd be prepared for Canada's wild, romantic winters. But, several weeks into our Canadian winter, after a hefty meal on his first night with us, he graciously declined to go for an after-dinner walk with us in the fresh snow.

We made our way around the block without our guest, blowing snowflakes from our faces and tossing snowballs at each other in the brisk night air. Drawing near the house, we stopped to stare, transfixed, into the window of the side bedroom we'd given our guest. There was Ade, dancing energetic circles across the floor in happy abandon.

Stomping the snow off our boots, we opened the door to rock music blasting from Ade's radio.

"Have a good time?" he greeted us, looking at our wet boots. "Me too. Got my big meal exercise too! And my feet are dry!"

Ade went to church with us on Sunday and showed great interest in comparing liturgy and traditions of our Canadian congregation with those of the Anglican Church that he had attended in Nigeria as a youngster and then in England where he went to upper school.

His sociological observations didn't stop there. We took him to visit suburban shopping malls and then downtown department stores. He studied store windows with special fascination.

"Stores in different countries have their own unique ways of attracting buyers' dollars. And attract buyers' dollars they surely do," he commented philosophically.

That year it was our family's turn to have Christmas dinner with my parents in the country. We knew he'd have a wonderful time there, noting our Christmas customs. I phoned Mom to say we had a Nigerian student as our Christmas week guest.

Silence. Then, a quiet little voice asked, "Nigeria. Is he...black?"

"Yes, Mom," I said, suddenly remembering that she'd been a young bride from a small town in 1924 when she first saw a black person. Knowing her small town, her new, urbane husband had pointed out a black person going into a store as he drove through the streets of the metropolitan city where they would start married life together. She had heard about people of different color but had never seen one until that moment. Her ignorance had embarrassed her.

Over the phone now, Mom cleared her throat and said hesitantly, "Oh dear, I've never talked to a black person, let alone over my own dinner table. What would I say? Does he speak English?"

Then, "Just a minute, let's see what Dad thinks," she said.

I relaxed. My stepfather, the son of an Anglican priest in Bermuda at the turn of the 20th century, enjoyed telling childhood stories. His love of the island's black inhabitants was obvious.

Mom returned to the phone, sounding more confident, "Dad says, of course, bring the young man for Christmas dinner. We'll give him a good time, good food and good talk."

On Christmas morning, we opened our gifts with Ade by our fireplace, his favorite spot in our house. As Ade went to his room to pack his new presents, our family slipped downstairs to pray about the Christmas dinner to be held at my parents' home that night.

We prayed Mom would be comfortable in this situation that was so new for her. We asked the Lord that this older lady, whose hospitable nature was one of her many wonderful traits, would be enabled to graciously welcome Ade. We expressed our faith that this Christmas celebration would be marked by much joy and happiness that everybody would remember years later.

A roaring fireplace and a host of lighted candles greeted us warmly as we stepped from the windy winter night into Mom and Dad's bright living room where hot apple cider waited.

As always, a crackling fire drew Ade and he warmed both his hands and his heart there. "Your home is so beautiful, so warm and welcoming!" said Ade with his wide grin and enthusiastically arching eyebrows.

The smile of appreciation on Mom's face at his words and the warm handshake Dad gave our young black friend augured well for the wonderful evening we were expecting and praying for.

And just how did the evening go? Ade's words expressed it best as we all filed back into our house, tired but happy.

"What a night! What a dinner!" he exclaimed. "What a warm, loving home! Your Dad...so knowledgeable, so wise. Such stories he had to tell! I couldn't hear enough about his life in Bermuda. Ah, and your mother... such a charming, beautiful hostess! She made me feel so much at home. I felt like a prince when she laughed at my 'first snow' story!"

I smiled as I imagined an angel taking notes: "Another big 'A' for the little woman with the big heart who became color-blind so she could freely extend true Christmas hospitality."

Beginning Where She Can Trust

God uses a friendly foot in the door to share His love

She sat on the edge of her chair in the doctor's office, purse clutched tightly on her lap, knuckles white.

"No, I won't tell you what's wrong with me," she answered the doctor, "That's your job!"

She was someone else's elderly mother, but she had asked me to take her to a doctor. The doctor and I tried in vain to reassure her and get her to describe her pain. She got up from her chair and flounced out of his office. At this point I was more concerned with her emotional state than I was with her physical condition.

She wasn't accepting anybody's help. I sensed that as she had been with the doctor, so she was with God. She needed God, she needed the doctor, and she needed me. But she'd tied our hands. This appointment was over, but it had served no purpose.

How does God feel when troubled people refuse His help? What did He think about this impasse?

The thought came, "She asked you to bring her to this appointment."

Yes, but what good had it done for her? She came to the doctor for his advice and then treated him like an enemy instead of someone to solve her problem. She was in pain. That was obvious. But why didn't her pain motivate her to open up about her symptoms? I couldn't see any way that I could help this deeply distressed little woman

I looked at her sitting in the car beside me as we crossed the city to get home. I knew her pain went far beyond the physical. I'd heard stories of the father who'd bullied her as a child. Then as a teenager she was married off to a farm hand who treated her as someone to clean house, make meals and raise children. Finally, as an unsupported woman, she brought up four children on her own after her husband left home. She harbored hate in her heart for men, especially for fathers. When I once spoke of "Father God" to her, it had fallen on disdainful ears.

"She asked you to take her to the doctor," the Lord reminded me, leading my thoughts.

Yes, I reflected, she did ask for my help. Even though I was no help to either her or the doctor today, she seemed to accept me, even lean on me a little.

"Let her see you being blessed by My Father love," said the Lord, moving me on to the next step.

Hmm, I thought, if she's open to me and if she sees how much God's caring love means to me, could she relate the care and help I give her with the Father God I look to for help when I need it?

"Her body is gravely ill but even more serious is her deeply injured soul," said the Lord. "You may never know what your kindness means to her. Let Me touch her with My love where she can trust at this point ...through you!"

It's wonderful at anytime to tell of the goodness of the Lord but it was especially so for me on this drive home, as I shared some difficult times in my life when I knew I needed help and God had answered my prayers.

This trip to the big city to visit her daughter had been full of conflict and hurt feelings for both of them, so my husband offered to drive the ill woman to the railway station when she wanted to get back home. He returned home with a surprise for me.

"You won't believe this," he said. "She didn't say a word all the way to the station. When we came to a stop in front of the entrance and I was about to reach for her bag from the back seat, she put a hand on my arm to stop me long enough to say, "Your wife was a good friend to me. Tell her, will you?"

Yes, I was surprised to hear that. What did my sharing mean to her journey out of this world? Why hadn't I led her to the Lord or prayed for her healing in the short time we had together? Would she have been ready for that?

Sometimes we are called to plant the seed (John 4:37). Sometimes we're called to cultivate it. Sometimes we get to reap the harvest. But we often never know the results of the obedience asked of us at any time. The reward for caring for others in His Name is simply serving this God who cares for each one of us, more than we can ever know or imagine.

A Wrestling Ring Can Change To A Prayer Corner

when we need help to be the caregivers our aging parents need

We had been planning and arranging for the day when Mom, now 91, would be ready to sell her home and move in with us. She would be our very special guest, honored and loved, fussed over and entertained.

I thought we had everything down pat. We would make our ensuite into her private apartment. The walls would display her own favorite pictures and the open shelving would hold her own beloved figurines. Our walk-in closet was emptied to accommodate her entire wardrobe from shoes of every shape to her three little gray wigs. We had thought out the best place for every stick of furniture she would bring with her. She would feel at home.

I wasn't prepared for her reaction to this last-stage move of her life. We meant well as we made all the arrangements for her to live with us, but something wasn't working right. There was friction in the house and we all knew it, but I didn't know what the source was.

The best way to handle this domestic disruption was to get the Lord's mind on this. I was sure I knew His heart, that she might be comfortable, peaceful and happy and that everything in her ensuite would be convenient for her living there.

Looking for the Lord's advice early one of many mornings, I curled up with pencil and paper on the living room sofa to hear the Holy Spirit's suggestions for my "projects" of the ensuite on Mom's behalf.

"On whose behalf?" the Holy Spirit said quietly.

"On whose behalf?" I repeated, somewhat bewildered, but surmising that the Holy Spirit wanted me to do some thinking.

"For whom do you want the arranging of the ensuite to be peaceful and convenient?" He asked.

"Oh for Mom, of course," I said. "This is all about her and her comfort."

"And what does she have to say about the positioning of furniture and pictures, the timing of getting up, having meals, going to bed at night and which of your guests she will come downstairs to meet?"

"I've been thinking about all that for the past year and I think I know what would be helpful for her in these circumstances," I said thoughtfully.

"These circumstances, you say," He said gently. "That is the point. These circumstances are circumstances she has never faced before and over which she feels she has no control. What does that mean to you?" the Spirit said, prodding me to think through our situation from Mom's viewpoint.

Ah, I thought, Mom's been used to being her own boss in her own house for six years since Dad died. And before that, she ran her own household to serve husband, children and visitors for over 40 years. This is a big change for her. And here I am, bustling about, dealing with every detail of her life without finding out what she sees as her needs and preferences.

"This is heavy. Lord, where do we go from here?" I asked, somewhat abashedly. "Should I start with the furniture? She's been living here a week and probably has some ideas of her own about how things could work better for her."

"That is a good idea to explore," said the Holy Spirit, the impression of His voice fading into the background.

Guess I'm on my own, then, I thought. Oh, that's what He was saying, this is not just about me! It's Mother's circumstances we're talking about. I should ask her if I could come up to her ensuite apartment after breakfast and see how the furniture placement is working for her. Is it too crowded by the window? Is it too hard to get in and out of bed with her desk so close to the headboard? How about the stool by the bathtub? Is that where it's going to be most useful?

I was off and running with questions rather than advice, suggestions rather than decisions. This was going to be fun. And I knew it was going to help Mom's transition from a life of independence to one of joint consultation. We'd start with the arrangement of her furniture as it would suit her and go on to other things like her favorite meals. I was excited. I was dissolving my well-meaning dictatorship in favor of a partnership through which I was going to learn a thing or two as the junior partner.

As for Mom's tendency to question our lifestyle and even some priorities that were especially important to us: that would take a few more pre-dawn consultations with the Lord. But at least my perspective had become something God could work with to bless my little Mom who was facing one of the biggest challenges of her life.

I smile as I remember the day Mom started to make a derogatory remark about a practice that came from a tradition other than her own. I thought, How can such a lovely lady come out with what she's starting to say?

"Lord," I prayed, "help!"

Mom stopped her remark in mid-sentence. "Well I guess I shouldn't criticize. I have to learn not to make remarks."

"Sounds good!" I smiled broadly at her. "Forget the remarks unless they are as positive, as helpful and as loving as you are!"

Her returning smile told me she understood I was honoring her and her discretion.

Over the next 12 years, Mom's ability to make good decisions for her own welfare declined and I sometimes had to look hard for things we could leave up to her to decide. But the Lord had stabilized for us the most important factor of living together. The partnership we established with our beloved house guest let us work things through together, even if the mantle of responsibility for her welfare grew bigger for me with each bout of pneumonia, each session with a broken limb, each minor stroke incident.

As the years passed and Mom grew more dependent, she also became more appreciative of our thoughtful care. I'll never forget the day she took the hands of her "caregiver" and of her "financial manager" in her own. As she smiled into our eyes, she said to my husband and to me, "What would I ever do without you two?"

What else could I say but, "And aren't we three blessed to have the best seniors' counselor there ever was and ever will be, the Lord Himself!"

Mary's Arrival

the Holy Spirit gives a glimpse into that waiting world

One morning, in that world halfway between sleeping and waking, the Lord gave me a precious picture. It was of my elderly mother whose 100th birthday was just weeks away. In it, I was watching Mom make the transition from eternal life that begins here on earth as we accept Jesus as our Savior and Lord, to the eternal life we will live in His closer presence after leaving this world. Scripture leapt out at me as I watched.

Mom's little, grey-haired self stood at the Great Portal of Heaven a little tremulously, eyes bright, eyebrows raised in anticipation, a smile about to break across her face as she gave a quiet knock at the door. Everything about the great entrance was warmly welcoming, as a friend's doorway seems when you know your arrival is awaited with happy expectation.

The door opened and a gentle throng of people drew her into an anteroom every bit as warmly welcoming. As loving voices surrounded her and kindly hands seated her, Mom tried, as she had for so many recent years, to focus on the words and the faces so she could tune in to what people were saying. After peering with concentration for several minutes at those around her, she smiled and made an aside, "You'll understand when you get my age."

Clouds of bright laughter went up from the inhabitants, some of whom had been there for hundreds of years as they returned her smile. And then a sudden expectant hush, as all attention was drawn to a regal looking door. The loving voices burst into joyous praise as the door swung open. Music, that Mom as girl church organist had never before heard, rose exquisitely, majestically, yet familiarly to fill the anteroom.

"Mary Elizabeth Madeleine, Roblin, McKenzie, Bilkey," called a voice that could only be described as All-Love. Warm hands, somehow familiar but never before quite so experienced, enfolded Mom's little, gnarled hands. She looked into eyes that were also somehow familiar, but once again, never before so experienced, and heard love pour out with the words, "Welcome, Mary!"

The cloud of loving sound billowed around Mom with praise and blessing as the loving hand of God raised her to her feet and drew her into arms that enveloped her with love familiar but never before so experienced.

"Oh I never knew it would be like this," she laughed and cried. "O, God, I love You. I've loved you for a long time but now I love You closer, so close I hardly dare breathe!"

She realized with gratitude that her focus was sharpening as she strove to understand everything going on around her. She was sure her vision was also sharpening as she continued to gaze into the eyes of her God. Then she saw Someone, somehow familiar but never before so experienced. She knew it must be Jesus smiling at her there at God's right hand (Acts 7:56).

She noticed her focus, now her hands, now her body were changing. In the twinkling of an eye it was happening (1 Corinthians 15:52). She began to move with grace and freedom. It felt so good. But best of all, was the singly-focused praise that burst from her lips with unfettered joy as she fell to her knees and clasped the feet of her Lord. With a smile, He drew her to her feet, saying, "Mary Elizabeth Madeleine, do you know you are home now?"

"Yes, yes, yes!" she laughed, twirling about on suddenly nimble toes with delight as she looked around at the beauty and grandeur opening up about her. "Yes, I know I'm home!" Then she whispered, "Jesus, how can I ever thank You for what You have done?"

Mary was quiet for a moment. Then she said earnestly, "Dear God, when You have time, I have so many things to ask You about that I don't understand."

That enveloping smile answered her as the Lord God of Heaven and Creation nodded.

Mary dearly wanted to talk to people around her who she was certain she recognized and whose names she was sure she was going to remember. But there was something she still had to do. She turned to look back through the big gate quietly closing.

"I'm now part of that Cloud of Witnesses who will be praying for you!" she said, blowing a kiss towards loved ones mourning her departure (Hebrews 12:1). Then she skipped off to talk to those familiar faces and find the place the Lord had prepared for her (John 14:2).

Indeed, Mary was home.

—☙—

Footnote: I hesitated to let Mom read this story because it was about her dying, until, at 103, she was declining physically very quickly. When I read it to her, she smiled at me like an indulgent mother. "That's beautiful. Would you please read that at my funeral one day?" she asked. Two weeks later I did and the joy of the Lord filled the chapel.

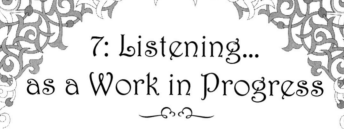

7: Listening...
as a Work in Progress

Not Perfect, Just On The Path

words with fists put a finger on the problem

As a young couple, my husband and I had become church-goers in a new suburban community. I accepted Jesus Christ with enthusiasm but didn't yet know I had a lot learn about this new life in Christ. My husband heard my pronouncements about my new-found faith and watched as I tried to walk my talk.

One day he confronted me in frustration. "I hear what you say but I see how you behave. You seem to see yourself as somehow perfect now that you've decided to become a Christian. But when I see what you do I wonder if God can really do anything with anybody!"

Sometimes words have fists. This was one of those times. God is not the author of hurtful words that come our way. But He can make use of criticism and words with fists if they can reveal to us things we are too blind or stubborn to recognize. It takes a heart open to His Spirit to get the point of what is being said no matter how it bruises our ego.

The accusation had been made: my mouth and actions spoke different things about my identity in Christ. How I faced that accusation would have a strong effect on my husband, just beginning his own journey to find God.

What made my husband's remarks so challenging was the fact that I was just back from a week-end retreat with fifty Christian women. Thanks to that week-end I was beginning to grasp who I was in Christ and what my spiritual heritage was. Thanks to that week-end, I discovered that God couldn't love me any more if I were the only child He had and that Jesus Christ's death meant I could become like His Son. I didn't understand all this completely, but I found God's plan more awesome than when I'd first heard and accepted it the year before. I realized I had a long way to go to be like Jesus and was full of zeal to get on with that journey. But somehow my husband interpreted my zeal as saying "I have arrived!" How could I come across like that after spending a week learning to sit at Jesus' feet and hearing what He has said about those who belong to Him?

That weekend I knew for sure that I belonged to Jesus. When I had first asked Jesus into my life, I'd found the Christian life pleasant and challenging. But I hadn't known in those early days that God wanted all of me. As this truth hit me that week-end a year later, I gave Him all I knew to give, asking Him to show me any part of me I'd missed surrendering to Him.

His answer was prompt and direct. It seemed He wanted my ego and had used someone who knew me very well to get that across to me.

My surrender at the retreat had been easy because Jesus had just won my heart completely as I saw His unconditional love for me. I would do anything for Jesus. Presenting my ego to Him, I heard His Holy Spirit speak in that gentle manner I have since come to expect and trust when I need correction: "Though you are not perfect, you are perfectly suited to the growth path I have set your feet upon."

His written Word that underlines this is found in James 1:2-4:

My brethren, count it all joy when you fall into various trials, knowing that the testing of your faith produces patience. But let patience have its perfect work, that you may be perfect and complete, lacking nothing (James 1:2-4).

The Price Of Success

does God ever plan birthday parties for three-year-olds?

I envied Betty. Everything she did seemed thoroughly appropriate, effective and in perfect taste no matter what was happening. Besides that, she had a mix of confidence and unselfconsciousness I wanted to emulate, without yet knowing the key to her success.

But I saw what made Betty tick as we planned the birthday party of her three-year-old. Arriving unexpectedly at my house one afternoon, in her warm, bright way she said she'd come for party ideas and pulled me down onto the sofa seat beside her to pray. In my new life as a Christian, I'd never seen anybody ask God to help plan a birthday party. Her transparent prayer intrigued me.

"Lord, You know the mess I make of things when I don't plan with You first. I don't know what to do for the party tomorrow because I haven't asked what You want yet. Please give us good ideas so the kids will enjoy themselves and their parents will see Your love at work. Thank You, in Jesus' Name."

Betty really expected God to make the difference between the fun or failure of a preschooler's birthday party. It hardly seemed a great spiritual adventure. I had questions and I asked them.

Betty laughed, "Just because I'm a schoolteacher doesn't mean I'm naturally organized and that I easily handle all the unexpected happenings in a classroom. I have to team up with the Lord before the school day begins or I'm lost. Actually, I try to remember to get His input for anything I do. Things go better when I let His love cover it all. That's John 15:4. It's called 'abiding'," she smiled. "Now, let's see what we three can come up with." And we prayed.

The party was a success. The little people were tired but glowing as parents came to collect them. As we tidied up, we shared memories of the kids' reactions to all we'd planned. But when Betty gave me a hug of thanks at the door, I said, "No, I thank you! I've discovered the cost of your success with people. You pay for it on your knees."

"That's always a good place to be," smiled Betty, "a good place to be."

—⚬⚬—

Music Memory, His Way

I get frustrated, but God has a fun solution

This is about a song I didn't want and couldn't get out of my head. You may know exactly what I mean. But on that day, God had a fun solution for me.

Since the Holy Spirit knows what is ahead for us (Revelation 1:8), we shouldn't be surprised to find a memo of encouragement or direction pinned up in our spirit, as it were, before some emergency situation arises in our day. For me, that can often come in the form of what I call a "Barnabas song" running through my head. Disciple Barnabas was called the encourager (Acts 4:36).

I always find out later just why the Holy Spirit has quickened to my memory some specific scripture or scriptural song that stays with me through a day of challenges.

I love waking in the morning to lyrics the Holy Spirit prompts to my mind such as, "I love You Lord, and I lift my voice to worship You, O my soul rejoice ..." or "Cause me to know Your loving-kindness in the morning, for in You do I trust."

But as I awoke this one particular morning, I found the wrong music playing in my head for a day that I knew would be full of challenges.

My dear mom living with us, was now in her 101st year and weak after a long, drawn-out cold. After she had several bad falls I called the doctor for an appointment and stayed alert for any unusual sounds from her room.

When her time came, we didn't want her to die short of breath or distressed by aches and pains from falls caused by dizziness provoked by infection. We wanted her to slip into heaven while asleep in sweet peace. This was our prayer and we held onto it.

This morning, we would be taking her frail little self out on this cold, windy, winter day to see the doctor for an assessment of her condition. We would have the car warmed, bundle her up against the weather and surround her with peace and gentle reassurance as we tucked her into her seat for the trip to the clinic.

This was not the morning to wake up to a catchy Italian love song running around in my head. The song had been driven into my head the previous day, as I'd listened to the radio while preparing lunch. The tune was no problem at the time. But on this particular morning, I wanted to fill my head with scriptural songs that would help me bless and support Mom as we went with our questions to her doctor.

This little nonsense song would not budge. I was not pleased. This distraction had nothing constructive to offer. And by no stretch of the imagination could it be a message from the Lord as it proclaimed: "When the moon hits your eye like a big pizza pie that's amore!"

Lying there on my bed that early morning, I tried replacing the ditty with an edifying spiritual song but fell back to sleep before succeeding. Minutes later, the musical confection started up again. This time I sat straight up in bed and shook a "spiritual fist" in the air as I declared, "Oh no you don't, you old deceiver, you're not going to rob me of the opportunity to sing out a strong, positive confession in the face of all we have to deal with today."

No, the Holy Spirit didn't prompt a spiritual song from my repertoire to replace that persistent little ditty. This little ditty had a catchy melody, so we went with it. Wide-awake now, I worked with the Holy Spirit's inspiration till the words formed in my head. But I could hardly sing for laughing: "When the Lord strengthens you and He carries you through, that's agape!"

Ah, just what we needed.

"I create the fruit of the lips: peace, peace to him who is far off and to him who is near," says the Lord, "and I will heal him (Isaiah 57:19).

In The Rustle Of His Garments

resting in His shadow, pressing close

In a difficult time, I talk with God as I wake to morning light.

"I have seen you pursued," says the Lord gently,
"as a small vulnerable creature of the woods,
stretching every nerve, every fibre of your being
to reach the safety of your den
and escape the very breath of your tormentor
even as you thought your own last breath was drawn.
Now you lie spent after the chase,
sprawled on your small, heaving side,
waiting for the trembling to stop,
too weary to think past the relief of your escape,
grateful for a next deepening breath,
the threatening presence of your enemy
shut out from this place of sanctuary.
I am here, My hand upon you.
Rest now in the stillness, the quietness.
Drink in My Peace."

"Lord," I respond, "I steal close to Your side
and rest in Your shadow.
I press as close as I can, to hide myself in You.
Arching my back like a small woods creature under
Your hand,
I draw on Your power, feel Your love pour over me.
Your life renews my strength.
I see Your smile, I hear Your voice
and I arise to walk in the rustle of Your garments."

An Accident Worth Remembering

praise on the highway freshens a spirit to counter a challenge

Not many people like remembering a car accident. But I do enjoy remembering one through which I learned an essential preparation for coming through an accident successfully.

It happened on one of the days I made my weekly visit to my elderly mother, now living alone in a city two hours away. I knew my husband had some concern over my frequent trips to see her, but agreed that at this stage of her life they were necessary until she was ready to come and live with us.

I also knew that my visits would be sprinkled with her regrets at having to one day leave her beautiful, wooded acreage. I loved Mom dearly and understood her despondence, though I sometimes felt a bit ragged around the edges as I left on my trip home. Our visit this day had been sprinkled with more regrets than usual. As I drove down the highway towards home, I turned to the Lord for His refreshing touch.

The best way I know to do that is to fill my car with songs of praise and rejoicing at God's loving care. But on this trip He seemed to be blessing me with a special sense of security, joy and peace as I sang out His praises and enjoyed His presence.

Nearing home, I was glad the trip was almost over as first snow flurries of the season slicked the highway's greasy surface. Driving in the outside lane, I left the requisite cautionary space between my car and the one ahead.

That cautionary space vanished as a car from the next lane careened in front of me. To avoid slamming into his rear fender, I made a quick left turn onto the highway shoulder. I held my breath as my car slid into the snow-covered median dividing me from oncoming traffic in the opposite direction.

With presence of mind that awed me in retrospect, I calmly pulled the key from the dead ignition, grabbed my parcels, locked the doors and was climbing up the median to the highway in a matter of minutes.

"Journey's End" read the brightly lit motel sign on the other side of the highway. Too right! I laughed to myself and prayed for a speedy, safe crossing over the four congested lanes of traffic to reach the motel and find help.

I watched amazed as traffic opened up like the waters of the Red Sea to let me sprint to the other side of the roadway and hike along the shoulder in the motel's direction.

I didn't have time to get to there. In the next moment, a huge transport truck drew up beside me and a young, black-haired and bearded driver opened the door of his cab and leaned over to call to me.

"Hi, there. Sorry it took me so long to cross to this lane, but you know what the highway is like tonight. Jump in. Can I help you get to where you're going?"

As I climbed up into the cab with my parcels, he smiled and gave me his hand, saying, "Saw your shadow crossing the four lanes. Then I spotted your car on the median and knew exactly what had happened. So tell me, are you okay? And where would you like me to drop you off?"

We were ten minutes from my house. In those minutes I discovered he was a Christian and had made many such rescues along North American highways in his career as a transport driver.

Safe at home once more, telling my husband about my close call and my knight-in-shining-transport-truck, I found myself thinking about the television series, "Touched by an Angel".

Whoever he was, my angel/knight was surely one sent by God for me on that trip. As I expressed my gratitude to the Lord and prayed for my rescuer out there on that greasy, treacherous highway this night, I vowed to never take a trip anywhere without first praising my Lord for His care or without getting defensively "prayed up" for any misadventure that might come my way on the road.

I've haven't seen that driver on the highway since that night, but I always peer up into the cab when I see an Erb Transport truck on the road. Wouldn't you?

"Cocky", Who Me?

God can help change a bad attitude

God does not always speak to man in long paragraphs, but sometimes He does. He does not always make a point with a simple impression upon our spirit, but at times He does. God does not always use a verse of scripture that seems to leap off the page, but often He does.

Nor does God always drop one, solitary word into somebody's mind to get somebody moving in the right direction. But I remember when He did that for me as a young Christian. The word was "Cocky," hanging there among my thoughts without any reference to any situation I was aware of.

Cocky. What was I to do with that word? I felt like a pupil standing in front of the teacher, asking what to do with an assigned problem I was supposed to solve.

Do you remember asking the teacher how to find an answer when she wanted you to work it through for yourself? There'd be no verbal reply, just the tucked-in chin and the slightly raised eyebrow that signaled you were to put on your thinking cap and apply what she'd already taught you.

Well, I felt a bit like that, so I took a deep breath and tried to think why the Lord seemed to be bringing this word to my attention. To start, Cocky is an adjective describing behavior. Behavior springs from attitude. Attitude speaks of the condition of the heart. God is concerned with my heart because it determines my attitude and my attitude determines my behavior. My behavior is supposed to model the behavior of Jesus.

Well, Cocky certainly doesn't apply to the way Jesus lived. I want my behavior to show Jesus. When I gave my heart to Jesus as Lord and Savior, one of the first things He saved me from was an attitude of self-deprecation that was lodged in my heart. The change didn't happen all at once. The Holy Spirit patiently worked with me to recognize and turn that wrong attitude over to Father God who had sacrificed His Son that I might have freedom in Christ.

Cocky attitude sounded very different from a self-deprecating attitude. I'd never thought of myself as smart-alecky or proud. Was this really God suggesting to me that it was time to deal with Cocky? I was surprised enough to put on my mental magnifying glasses to scrutinize this attitude. Two Scriptures flew to mind giving me a clear view of how I should be standing before my Teacher, the Holy Spirit.

Search me, O God...and see if there is any wicked way in me (Psalm 139:23).

Every way of a man is right in his own eyes, but the Lord weighs the heart (Proverbs 21:2).

This all should have been freeing me to call on the Lord for His help but because I was self-focusing it only depressed me. I laughed at myself a bit (which can be good if you're taking yourself too seriously) by coining a phrase, "Self analysis can be paralysis". Then wanting to stand before my Teacher with the right posture, I repeated that promise from God in Jeremiah 29:13, 14:

You will seek Me and find Me when you search for Me with all your heart. I will be found by you and I will bring you back from your captivity (Jeremiah 29:13, 14).

With all my heart I do seek Him, I thought. His promise is that He will bring me back from the captivity of my self-focusing. Now that I can see that, self-focus looks pretty cocky! Praise God that Psalms and Proverbs, so full of the human condition, always point us to God's Spirit for answers, if we choose to listen and hear. I was eager to listen and I wanted to hear, so I memorized those verses from Psalm 139 and Proverbs 21 to have that scriptural wisdom instantly available whenever, wherever I need it.

Choosing to look objectively at my life for the purpose of detecting cockiness and self-focus in my behavior, I cringed to remember some (now) embarrassing times when I'd felt that I knew better than somebody else and had defensively paraded my "superior knowledge" with aggravating pride. Indeed that was "Cocky". I suspected I could be Cocky anytime the occasion allowed, unless I put Cocky into The Lord's hands now that I had recognized it as an odd by-product of self-deprecation.

"Lord," I said, "You've seen 'Cocky' in me. You've faced me with it and I repent of it. I dump this burden of Cocky at Your feet right now. The only pride I have is in the fact that Jesus loved me so much He died for me so I could be free and grow to be like Him. To be like Jesus is a big order. With the help of Your Holy Spirit, I'll work on that until Christ returns."

—◌◌◌—

The day the Lord had me take that "class" on Cocky, my husband and I were to attend a home group leaders' meeting at our little church in the suburbs. I found myself wondering if Cocky could refer to anybody who would be at tonight's meeting. Just who was Cocky? I groaned as I got out of the car to go into the meeting. What if I was able to spot Cocky all over the place tonight?

His answer came as I raised my hand to knock on the door, "What is that to you? You follow Me!"

"What Is It?" The Lord Says

He doesn't ask what I want

Pulling the blanket close around my aching body in this hospital bed, I know where I'm supposed to be. I'm supposed to be in a place where I can pray. I need to pray right now and with conviction as the emergency room doctor's words, "danger of flesh-eating disease in this leg", strike fear in my heart. But the distance to the hospital chapel is just too far for me to navigate at this point.

I tell myself that I don't need to be in some special place to pray. I just need to start praying. I can and do imagine myself as going into God's Throne Room in Heaven to tell Him my problem and to ask for His help. I know He's the answer to infection ravaging my injured leg, spacing me out. So I stagger weakly into His Throne Room, as it were, to wait before Him.

The loving-kindness in His voice is like the touch of a soothing hand as He addresses me, "What is it, My Child?"

I think a minute. God knows everything. He knows I need His help. He hasn't asked me, "What do you want?" He has said, "What is it?" Why does the Lord ask me what is it that brings me to Him in prayer when He knows everything about me? He must be asking me to clarify what is it, for my own sake. Well, I know for sure that this stay in the hospital for blood poisoning and infection is turning out to be a battle.

"And the battle is the Lord's!" I respond as my spirit asserts its rightful control as director over my mind, will and emotions, to declare my faith before God.

"Lord," I thank Him, "You have given Your children Your authority and power, through Jesus' precious blood, shed on the cross of Calvary. In the name of Jesus, we can pray that Your will be done.

"With this authority that is mine as a believer," I say, wielding the sword of the Spirit which is the Word of God, "I command Satan, the enemy of my soul, to stop right there in Jesus' mighty Name. You have no business harassing a daughter of the King. And I am a daughter of the King[1]. Not only will you come no further, you will cease and desist. You will turn and flee. And because I know that my healing is through the precious blood of Jesus so I can, and do, claim that healing in His Name."[2]

Then with a big sigh of gratitude, I thank God for His encouragement and strengthening to deal with my fear of a bad outcome to my medical emergency.

"You have rightly said what it is. It is a battle. My Son has won that battle and you have your victory through His blood and in His Name."

I hear God's reassuring affirmation in my heart and give Him my praise.

Now it's time to step out of the prayer room of my heart and resume my role as patient of the hospital's medical

1. Isaiah 33:22
2. Acts 3:16.

staff to whom I am submitted. I submit to them with every confidence, since I've already submitted them to the Lord for His wisdom in all they do for me.

My healing from that condition doesn't come instantly. It takes months. These are months for which the Lord gives me comfort, patience and confidence every step of the way until my healing is completed. During these months I cherish the time to think and marvel at what the Lord is doing for me.

I recognize Jesus as the most integrated personality the world has ever known or will ever know. His spirit, always in communion with His Father God, was always in control of every circumstance He met, even if it didn't look like it at the time. When that great miracle worker was dying on the cross, He knew the victory He was winning, the salvation He was securing, for all those who believe that He conquered sickness, disease and sin on that day of all days.

What is it? I never tire of saying, "The battle is the Lord's and He has won it."

What is it? The battle is the Lord's and "we are more than conquerors through Him who loved us" – Romans 8:37.

Believers who trust in Jesus' Name will see the victory He won for us as we wield "the sword of the Spirit which is the Word of God" (Ephesians 6:17).

Thanks be to God Who gives us the victory through our Lord Jesus Christ (1 Corinthians 15:57).

He has redeemed my soul in peace from the battle that was against me (Psalm 55:18).

Please, I Want To Be A Blessing, Not A Cursing

a check in the spirit deals with an insensitive comment

Did you ever want to bite your tongue, especially when the Holy Spirit gets on your case? It turned out to be my case when I was stopped by a young friend as I left church one day.

The young man had something important to share and he was sharing it with me, supposedly the older and wiser for my years as a Christian.

He spoke in the hushed tone people use when they have something special to share: "I think God just told me He trusts me."

He waited for my response. What he got was my reaction...a wrong one. I didn't realize that as I spoke, but it drained away his new-found encouragement just the same.

"I believe God wants us to know He loves and accepts us," I pontificated, "but the only one He really trusts is Jesus,"

One look at his face told me my reply had been exactly the wrong one. The tentative little gleam of assurance I'd seen in his eyes as he had approached me faded as I said those words. I felt a sting of compunction as the Holy Spirit pointed out to me that I had been insensitive to this young man's need for encouragement in the Lord.

There had been a certain truth in my comment: who is truly trustworthy without being in sync with the Holy Spirit? But oh, why hadn't I waited for the Holy Spirit to show me what was going on in his heart so my words could minister life instead of an apparent put-down? At least I was able to save his sense of worth somewhat by reminding him of the times the Lord had brought victory out of apparent failure when he had submitted his problems to God and had done what he was told. But it was a while before I saw that gleam of assurance return to his eyes.

That was over 30 years ago. I've since learned to listen closely both to people and to the Holy Spirit as I consider what God wants spoken in any situation. I don't want to simply react with some comment off the top of my head.

That check in my spirit kept me praying for my young friend's security in the Lord and often speaking of God's love and expectations over his life at a particularly crucial time of change he was going through.

Jesus' concern about the care we give one another is obvious in Matthew. 25:40, "Inasmuch as you did it to the least of these My brethren, you did it to Me" and in Mark 9:42, "Whoever causes one of these (little ones) who believe in Me to stumble, it would be better for him if a millstone were hung around his neck."

—◦◦◦—

What about the blunders we make? What about the times we end up being more of a cursing than a blessing to someone? The best remedy for "misspeak" is making a beeline to my prayer room to get His wise and loving correction for future reference.

I like learning by seeing things work well. I like watching Jesus walk and live and minister in the New Testament. He did all things well. He had the right touch and He had it every time. We have that right touch when we keep close connections with His Spirit, the best Human Relations Consultant and Enabler to ever minister on this planet.

A favorite saying of teacher Agnes Sanford was from John 15:4 and Philippians 2:13: "Abide in me more and more, teaching me to will and do your good pleasure." I'd add, "may it truly be Your good pleasure because my pleasure isn't always so good!"

You Need An Ego To Sing

yes...and no.

"You have to know you're a somebody. You need an ego to sing!"

My friend was a professional singer and not a Christian. At the moment she looked as though she wanted to shake me.

Actually her words had shaken me already. I was to sing the solo part of the Sanctus during the communion service the next Sunday. How could I reconcile what my friend said with our Lord's words about self-denial?

I was a young Christian and the Holy Spirit had been teaching me, as a young wife and mother, how to live for Jesus and keep Him at the centre of my thoughts and actions. Now how could I possibly stand and sing with "ego" at the sacred high point of the sacrament? I was in psychological conflict. Often used Christian terminology such as "death to self", "throne of my life" and "self-abasement" fought in my mind with the need to stand and deliver a song with effectiveness and conviction.

For the next few days, I read and mused over some particular Scriptures, especially the passages, "Let him deny himself, take up his cross and follow Me" and "Without Me you can do nothing". Still confused, I sank into the big old cane rocker by my window.

"Help, Lord," I said simply.

No bolts from the blue. Not even a still small voice. Just a sense of being much loved and a joy at being able to serve so great a high priest. I rested there in His love, knowing it surrounded me and filled me. "Abide in Me, and I in you," Jesus had said in John 15:4.

Of course. "Yes, Lord," I said.

Sunday found me abiding in the Lord by faith alone. I managed to put my choir collar on backwards and then to drop all my music as I reached the choir loft. Even as the organist struck up the introductory chords of my solo, Satan whispered, "Now we'll see if it really works."

"Not 'it'", I declared, "but 'He'..."

I knew I was somebody, even as my friend had insisted. Somebody, that is, in God's hand. My ego, like my heart, was pulsing, beating for Christ. My voice rose in love for this holy Lord who had reminded me so simply, without condemnation, that when I had given Him my life, I had given Him my ego too. As the last note faded away, I thanked Him silently. I had just helped those taken communion this morning to honor our Lord together.

Ego? God knows about egos. I don't need anybody's intellectual exercises on the matter. I'll let God have my ego. He knows what to do with it.

"Unfruit"

the Holy Spirit's word game helps me walk in the Spirit

As a very young Christian, I was trying to get into God's Throne Room, in a manner of speaking, for comfort and peace after a particularly rough battle between my flesh and my spirit.

"Oh Lord," I sighed. "I'm new to this Christian life. Half the time I don't know if I'm walking in my flesh or in my spirit. Just when I think I'm getting my act together, doing what Your Word says, I find myself in a fit of temper or nursing a hurt if someone I want to help, rejects me."

I had come to Him like a preschooler who comes to his parent every time he falls, to have everything made better. But God seemed to be expecting something from me. Had I figured out what it was I wanted to ask of Him?

Well, I wanted Him to show me a fail-safe way to know whether I was functioning with my spirit in control or only thinking I was. Just starting to learn scripture so I could live by His Word, I'd read in Ephesians 6:17, 2 Timothy 2:15 and Hebrews 4:12 that the Word of God is the sword of the Spirit, rightly dividing between flesh and spirit. That's what I needed, a word from the Word that would rightly divide between walking in the flesh or the spirit.

I'd hardly thought that through, when the Holy Spirit dropped the word, "unfruit" among my thoughts.

But, but... I thought, 'unfruit' isn't in the Bible is it?

But the Lord hears our thoughts and the quiet reply came at once, "No, but 'fruit' is."

I like word games, but this didn't seem like a game. God wanted me to get a grip on His work standard. I pored over Galatians 5:22, 23 that talks about the fruit we bear and decided to adopt the words "fruit" and "unfruit" as a two-word alert to help me distinguish between works of the spirit and works of the flesh.

I began to identify anything that wasn't fruit as "unlove", "unjoy", "unpeace" etc. I didn't want to produce any unfruit to pass along to anyone. Believers walking in His Spirit bear fruit that blesses, only blesses. That's clear, I thought. If I'm walking in the spirit with His Spirit I'll be a blessing.

Lord, I thought, You've introduced me to a great word game. It's a "keeper" and I'm going to keep it.

Turn Down The Cold

God can't use double-minded prayer warriors

My head said I should somehow find a way to help this difficult person, but my heart wanted to back off.

Asking me for help, as I served on our church after-service prayer team, this visitor obviously needed to know that God loved her and wanted to bring healing into her challenging situation. But her negative attitude was working against her. She told me flatly that the Bible was no longer relevant and that she was sure God wouldn't waste His time trying to help her.

Then why, I wondered, was she asking for prayer if she didn't think God would answer her need. She may be looking for a sympathetic ear, but she certainly isn't looking for God's help, I told myself with more than a touch of irritation.

My own negativity shocked me and I reigned myself in to make a quick trip to my own personal prayer room in my heart. Even as I stood beside her, I was silently pleading with God, "You've helped me love difficult people before, but this time I'm really frustrated. This woman needs You. I'm sorry for her. I want to pray with her. But if she's not interested in Your help, where do we go from here?"

His answer pulled me up short: "Your heart and head are not in agreement. I can't use you when your soul is in a divided state like this."

The Lord is right, I thought. He's always right. I want to help but I find her quite impossible.

"I don't see her as impossible," the Holy Spirit said quietly. "I can take 'impossible' out of her heart, out of her mind, away from her expectations, though she too thinks she is impossible and communicates that to everyone around her. Remember, she doesn't know how much I love her yet.

"As for you, My daughter, God's love within you can love the seemingly impossible ones. But your own attitude right now is chilling anything I can do through you. It's your choice. Can you turn down the cold? Can you drop that negative attitude into My hands and let My love in you rise to bless her?"

Drop it I did, right then and right there. I looked at the woman beside me and saw with His eyes, not an impossible one, but a beloved one. God knows her name, I thought. God's Spirit in me loves her. I want to know her name.

She looked surprised that I was interested in knowing her name, since I must have given evidence by my cool manner that I was turned off by her attitude. She put her head down and said, "Marcy. My name is Marcy."

I took her hands, not stopping to think that she might pull away and wonder what I was doing. "Marcy," I said, sensing God's love pouring over her, amazing her, amazing me. "God loves you. And right now He's asking you to trust Him. You'll find He's true to His Word and His plans for you go far beyond anything you have hoped or dreamed."

I opened up my companion Bible to James 1:5-8 and asked if we could agree with this scripture since it seemed to speak to the difficult situation she had shared with me. I caught a glimmer of hope in her eyes as we read,

If any of you lacks wisdom, let him ask of God, who gives to all liberally and without reproach and it will be given to him. But let him ask in faith, with no doubting, for he who doubts is like a wave of the sea, driven and tossed by the wind. Let not that man suppose that he will receive

anything from the Lord; he is a double-minded man, unstable in all his ways (James 1:5-8).

I chuckled to myself, today I chose to not be double-minded and I'm glad I did.

No sooner had I thought that, when I heard Marcy say, "I don't want to be a double-minded person, but what if I'm not sure what God is going to do?"

"You have a choice, Marcy. You can expect the worst and turn your back on His help," I said, "or agree with His Word we just read, that tells us that if we ask and believe, He will give us the wisdom we need. You'll find Him true to His word. Everyday, I and so many other believers find that He is faithful to His Word. Why not step out and test Him too, Marcy?"

Marcy did that, laying her problems and hopes before Him, asking Him to forgive her for doubting Him, and to please give her wisdom for her situation.

Then Marcy asked if we could keep in touch, "for a little while, until I can get on my feet and start running after God, like the rest of you here are doing," she smiled a little wistfully, looking at the team in action around us, praying for people.

"But you are my sister in Christ," I said, "sisters keep in touch!"

Later that night I opened the same chapter of James for myself, poring over the dramatic truths of verses 19 to 25 the Lord was quickening to me:

So then my beloved brethren, let every man be swift to hear, slow to speak, slow to wrath: for the wrath of man does not produce the righteousness of God...He who looks into the perfect law of liberty and continues in it and is not a forgetful hearer but a doer of the work, this one will be blessed in what he does (James 1:19, 25).

I turned out the night light and sank under the covers with a big smile. "Amen and amen! That word is for my new sister and it's for me too!"

"Hunker Down"

the Holy Spirit knows how to get through to us

The Lord knows how much I love cats and in answer to my prayer for guidance, gave me this wonderful picture of a lion, muscles rippling under its sleek body, crouched close to the ground, watching, planning his next move according to the developing scene before him.

"Hunker down", whispered the Holy Spirit, "hunker down".

That's what that big cat is doing, I thought, watching with respect and admiration at the stance the beast was taking, purposed, alert, deliberate, focused.

1 Peter 5:8 speaks of the devil walking about like a roaring lion seeking whom he may devour. But Revelation 5:5 says of Jesus, "Behold the Lion of the tribe of Judah". Satan is only "like" a roaring lion but believers can remind themselves that he's the counterfeit, all roar and no teeth because Jesus pulled them all out.

But oh, to see Jesus, that Lion of Judah, hunkering close to the ground, waiting, poised, ready to spring at the precise moment to pin down the foe, to protect the lair and to win the meal. Jesus' meat and mine, is doing the will of the Father (John 4:34 KJV).

What a powerful metaphor: the lion hunkers down with patience to watch and to determine when, how and where wisdom will rule the next move. So if wisdom requires patience then patience, in turn, must have wisdom. God will give me both as I ask His enabling and am diligent to apply it.

Thank You, Lord. You know just what I need, just when I need it, just the way I can receive it.

Do All "Good" Prayers Go To Heaven?

the Holy Spirit breaks in on my prayer time

In my dream, I'm hard at work,
down on my knees, praying with grave concern.

In the middle of it all, a Voice speaks,
"Daughter, I'd like to break in here for a moment.
You can get back to all that shortly."

"Pardon? Is that You, Lord?" I ask.

"Yes, Child. Now these words: where are they going?"

"They're supposed to be going to You, Lord.
Aren't they coming in up there?"

"Actually, nothing's arrived here as yet.
But I do see you on your knees, working hard,
poring over your concerns."

"I'm on my knees alright, Lord,
but if nothing is coming through up there,
what could be going wrong?"

"Child, it's good you want to bring me your concerns,
but relationship comes first, doesn't it?
Without relationship, there is no communication.

I don't take you for granted.
I'm here, waiting to share My heart with you,
waiting for you to share your heart with Me."

"Lord, you know when I was a new Christian
I'd never bring You my concerns
without telling You how much I loved You first.
I miss just being quiet with You, Lord.
It's a privilege I don't get to (sigh) enjoy much anymore,
having so much to do all the time.
Thank You for reminding me that I just get too busy sometimes.
I'm going to seek Your presence
before I bring any more of my concerns."

"It's in My presence, that your concerns find answers," says
the Lord.

A Bridge, Not A Doormat

God wants the one, not the other

As I pondered the hard lesson my friend had learned after confusing servanthood with servility, the Holy Spirit gave
this picture-parable that contrasts a bridge with a doormat.
His touch of humor underlined the fact that it's the Lord
we're to take seriously, not ourselves.

A bridge takes people from one place to another.

A doormat goes nowhere.

A bridge gets washed clean by the rain.

A doormat gets dirty shoes wiped on it and often
gets beaten.

A bridge is resilient under traffic and gets repaired when necessary.

A doormat gets worn out and when worn out, thrown out.

With high visibility and easy access, a bridge attracts many to cross it to reach their destination.

Few people bother with a doormat except to snarl at it when they trip across it.

Jesus is mankind's bridge to God's love. As His followers, we become bridges in His Name washed, repaired when necessary, resilient, approachable, attracting people to the Way of the Lord. As bridges bearing His Name, we take people with their burdens to the best possible destination: the life-changing presence of God.

So I'm Intense!

God uses us the way He made us (1)

"Don't be so intense!"

Friends say that to be helpful. Perhaps they fear you'll burn out too soon.

But what if you *ARE* an intense person, like Saul of Tarsus, tuned to a higher (not necessarily finer) frequency than some, for who knows what purpose?

"Relax, okay fella? Relax, why don'tcha?"

Perhaps that affable direction is well meant, but perhaps, for you, it would mean missing God's direction.

God gives us, each one, our own special "frequency" with which to tune into His Holy Spirit. Whether we are intense or more relaxed, His intention is to use us, each one, according to His making and His plan

Disciple Andrew seemed an easy sort. Saul/Paul was a hyper type. What mattered was how God used each of them as they kept tuned into His will.

That goes for you as well. (Me too!)

No Jolly Green Giant

God uses us the way He made us (2)

Looking a little sheepish, but managing a casual amble, a young friend approached me after church one Sunday to say, "Since you give a prophetic word sometimes, maybe you can clue me in on what I think I'm hearing.

"I thought I had a word to give during the service this morning but I thought, naw, God doesn't talk like commercial television. On the other hand, it spoke to me. Do you suppose it could have been God?"

"What was the message?" I asked.

"Well," he said, "These words were just there in my head during worship time and I thought at first it might have been a prophecy from the Holy Spirit. But God wouldn't use words like that!"

"Words like what?" I asked.

"Well," he said, "if I remember it like I think I heard it, it went something like this: "Look up, look up. This is not the

Jolly Green Giant bringing in the peas for canning. I am real. I am your God, the Lord, Who hears your prayers, knows your pain, and wants you to bring all your troubles to Him. I am your Lord. I love you. Look up, look up, keep looking up!"

"But that's great!" I beamed. "That word from the Lord says we are to keep expecting help from God. It edifies, encourages and comforts. It supports Scripture like any prophetic word will do. You don't have to wonder about the style of language that prophetic word came in. God knows us. He usually uses expression natural to each person He wants to speak through," I went on, warming to my first little lecture on giving prophecy.

"He can choose any believer filled with His Spirit to speak by His Spirit if that believer is willing and obedient. Don't feel badly about missing this opportunity. Just decide to speak out the next time God has something for you to give. But judge any word you get before you give it. If it's from God, it'll check out with the scriptural picture of God's character and the message will agree with scriptural truth. Revelation 19:10 says that the testimony of Jesus is the spirit of prophecy. It's good to know any message any of us brings is to be biblically judged by leaders of our church (1 Corinthians 14:29).

"There," I said, taking a big breath. "After this little crash course on prophecy I'll have to get you some related scriptures."

My young friend had to crack a little parting joke, "And I don't even have to be Balaam's ass, eh?"

* Some related scriptures: 1 Corinthians 12, 1 Corinthians 14, Psalm 139: 17-18, Psalm 81:10, 1 John 4:1-2.

The story of Balaam's little talking donkey is found in Numbers 22:28.

Grandma's Broken Heart Learns "Whosoever" Love

God doesn't let traditional bias derail a loving spirit

Grandma Amelia was special. Jesus loved her and loved through her too. But she told me very plainly that God had something against her.

How could God have something against this dear person who had made Jesus the Lord of her life? He was that Jesus God had sent into the world "that whosoever believes in Him should not perish, but have everlasting life" (John 3:16). But from my Grandma's own mouth I had heard it: God hated something in her.

We loved Grandma Roblin. She came to stay with our family when I was in my teens. She visited other relatives after Grandad died, but we felt her home was with us. I'd visit her in her sunroom and we'd chat, share poetry and jokes until she sent me off to do my homework. I always felt homework could wait. Grandma seemed so frail these days. I took every opportunity to be with her.

One day she shared a poem, "Crossing the Bar", about putting out to sea for a distant shore to be with God. I began to understand as she talked, that crossing the bar was a poetic way of talking about dying. "Shed no tear for me when I have crossed the bar," she recited.

"It's so beautiful, Gram, but so sad," I whispered.

"You will read it at my funeral," she said, taking my hand, "and sing my favorite hymn, 'Abide with Me. I fear no foe with Thee at hand to bless. Ills have no weight and tears no bitterness,'" she sang softly, unevenly, yet with certainty. "'Where is death's sting? Where grave thy victory? I triumph still if Thou abide with me.'"

I still feel the soberness, the tenderness, the importance of those moments in Grandma's room, her eyes smiling into mine, unafraid, knowing where she was going.

Then came the shock. In that same quiet voice she said, "I have been wicked, child. I have hated people God loves but God gave me a second chance. It came when I had to go to St. Joseph's Hospital a while back. You know...I wasn't well and they had to find out what was wrong.

"St. Joseph's is a Catholic Hospital of course. I never liked Catholics. I was raised in a home where Catholics weren't liked. That doesn't excuse me, but it helps explain me," she smiled with a little shake of her head. "We make our own choices to love people created and loved by God or to hate them. 'If someone says he loves God but hates his brother, he is a liar; for he who does not love his brother whom he has seen, how can he love God whom he has not seen?' That's Scripture dear," she said, tapping my hand lightly, "first letter of John, chapter four, verse 20.

"Now when I was sent to St. Joseph's, I steeled myself against the hands of those nurses and nuns who laid hold of me to move me and wash me and wheel me around. I hated it. But they saw my pain and fear and just took care of me and loved me. My God gave me a love for those beautiful people who did all they could to help me be comfortable and have a little peace in my body.

"I have seen God among the Catholics and I have asked Him to forgive me for my attitude. He let me come to know them and let them take care of me with such kindness that it broke my heart for the hard feelings I'd harbored against them.

"Dear, you know I'm to return to St. Joseph's, and this time you won't see me return. But you remember that I'm in good hands: God's hands and the hands of those dear people at that hospital.

"Now." said my little Grandma, sitting as tall as possible. "One day not too far away, my funeral will be celebrated and you will sing that hymn I want you to sing and you will read that poem I want you to read," she smiled, sending me off to my homework.

Her impact on my mind and heart remains. Our God who loves across cultures, had given His daughter Amelia a special opportunity to love as He loved. And as He did, He broke a hard place in Grandma's heart that had to be broken if she were to love His way.

Two years after Grandma went to Heaven, I attended university. There I met the personable assistant sports editor of my university's student newspaper. From a Ukrainian background, his traditions were engagingly different from my own beloved Scot-Irish conventions. Right after graduation I married this man the Lord chose to be my husband.

As reporter on the newspaper of a small multicultural town I reveled in my first fulltime job, enthusiastically writing of the diverse cultures and thinking that abounded there. I loved it all.

I gave my life to Jesus Christ 14 years after that sunroom visit with Grandma, where I had experienced such a rush of God's love for all the "whosoevers" that Gram had come to love too. Through her, the Lord had given me a foretaste of that "whosoever love", even before I had met Him for myself.

Just how seriously Jesus views our acceptance of others, shows in the dramatic parable he told to impress on believers the need to surrender to Him any down-the-nose attitudes towards others we may harbor.

And if your eye causes you to sin, pluck it out and cast it from you. It is better to enter into life with one eye, rather than having two eyes to be cast into hell fire (Matthew 18:9).

Those are the words of the One who loves without prejudice. He commands us to do the same and gives us the grace to learn love like Jesus loves.

One day my Grandma is going to introduce me to her friends there in Heaven, from every race, every tribe and every place under the sun. Jesus Himself will be standing there in the midst, embracing them all.

Song In The Night

music when you need to remember what He said

"It's me again, Lord," I sighed. "I did well with Your help last month, until today, that is. So here I am, lugging in the same problem," I said, settling woefully into the big rocker and pulling my robe around me against the chill night air as the rest of the house slept.

"Same problem, same answer," hung the words among my thoughts.

"Oh, Lord, when things started to heat up again, I forgot what You said. Do you ever give little songs to remind people what You tell them? That would be good," I said, perking up at the idea.

But the Holy Spirit was ahead of me. "Your song begins," He said, "with 'Trust, praise, wait on the Lord...'"

The song on the next page came straight from the Holy Spirit to my heart that night (Psalm 42:8). Its gentle little waltz tune goes running through my head whenever I need to remember its message.

This first song the Lord gave me was just the one to plant in my heart. It became very dear because it was from the Lord and conveyed what I needed to hear.

Years later, thanking Him yet again for my little song of love, I wondered why He hadn't given me the kind of minor, searching, Hebraic melody I so love. I smiled in agreement as the Lord reminded me how young in my faith I had been at the time. Might I not have boasted over a wistful soaring melody, impressed by "my" first song, instead of delighting in the message that came on its wings? (The Lord did give me a lovely, wistful, song some years later when I could handle the beauty of it as being birthed by Him, not by me.)

Page Of Music:

Trust, Praise, Wait on the Lord

That song in the night

C   C7   C6   C
Trust, praise, wait on The Lord,

C   Dm   G
Let this be my delight.

Dm   Dm+7 Db7   G
Trust, praise, wait on The Lord,

G   Dm   G C
Early or deep in the night.

C   C7   C
Early each morning before yet the dawn

C   C   Cm Dm G
Let my spirit establish my song.

Dm   Dm+7   Dm7
All through the day when the mischiefs abound

Dm   G   C
Let my heart with Your praises resound.

```
C          G            C6
And in night watches when fears rise to slay

Cb7        F    A   Dm
Let my soul rejoicing yet say,

D    Dm7   Db7       G
Trust, praise, wait on The Lord,

G          Dm G  C
Let this be my delight.
C     C7    C6          C
Trust, praise, wait on The Lord,

C          Dm        G
Let this be my delight.

D    Dm7   Db7       G
Trust, praise, wait on The Lord,

G    Dm   G   C
Early or deep in the night.
```

───୧୨───

Stand Tall, Flat On Your Face

the Holy Spirit uses a cartoon to make it clear

The Holy Spirit once used a cartoon to get my attention when I was trying so hard to live the Christian life that I couldn't see past my own striving. As a new Christian, I was tying myself in knots trying to be vigorous in faith and appropriately humble at the same time.

My perspective obviously needed adjusting. I thought I should just stop everything I was trying to do and go to prayer, to ask God where I was going wrong.

When I did, the Holy Spirit sent me the picture of a lively stick figure dancing about, waving its arms with exuberance across the screen of my mind. That must be my spirit rejoicing in God's Spirit, I thought as I checked out Scripture on joy in my Bible's concordance to find,

And now may the God of Hope fill you with all joy and peace in believing, that you may abound in hope by the power of the Holy Spirit (Romans 15:13).

Then another little stick figure appeared. I thought it looked like it was having a temper tantrum, lying flat on its face there on the floor. But I soon saw it had joyfully spread itself out on the floor to signal its submission to the spirit within me. That must be my soul rejoicing in God's Spirit, I thought as I checked out Scripture again, this time on joy in my Bible's concordance to find,

My soul shall be joyful in the Lord, it shall rejoice in His salvation (Psalm 35: 9).

The big smiles on the faces of both stick figures showed their joy in the Lord, but their ways of expressing it were so different.

I laughed. In the middle of something the Holy Spirit was teaching me, I could laugh? Well, I was getting the point the Holy Spirit was making. Both figures were expressing joy in the Lord. What looked at first like a paradox, was healthy spirituality in both instances. The first stick character represents my spirit, perfect in Jesus, standing tall and praising, ready to boldly lead wherever God directed. The second character, flat on its face, must be my soul with mind, will and emotion submitted to the Lord in humility and serenity, happily following orders from His Spirit within my spirit.

I treasure the memory of that cartoon that helped me find God's balance for my life, with my spirit, born of His Spirit, taking the lead in all things and my soul, happily following my spirit's orders.

And no, I can't say I take myself too seriously anymore.

⌒ઉⱅ⌒

When? When!

God gives the answers, gently but firmly

"When am I going to get some real responsibility?" I complain.

"When," says the Lord, "you learn to recognize My Lordship over your every thought, word and deed."

"When are people going to take me seriously?" I sulk.

"When," says the Lord, "I become more important to you than anything or anybody in your life."

"When am I going to get a little respect around here?" I wail.

"When," says the Lord, "you come to respect My will for you and My concern for others."

"When are people going to see I'm worth something?" I cry.

"When," says the Lord, "you live your life so they can see My Son Jesus living His life in all you do."

"O Lord," I weep, "let me be real!"

"You are as real," says the Lord, "as you are obedient to reveal My Truth in all you do."

"Dear God, how can I please you?" I whisper.

"Listen to My Spirit," says the Lord...and hold still long enough to let Me love you!"

(Matthew 18: 3, 4; 23: 12; John 14:21, 23; James 4: 6, 10)

Centre Of Whose Universe?

an exuberant kitten demonstrates "hallel" praise

As parents of adult offspring, we've learned to respect the diversities that developed in the lives of our children after leaving home. Our son grew up in a cat aficionado house but became a dog lover. That might help explain his response to the new kitten we took into our home and hearts. His amused consideration of our new family member gave me this real life parable.

Shortly after little Taffy became part of our household, our son came to visit and found his Dad, Mom and Grandma acting a bit silly over this new and highly active ginger kitten.

"That little cat," he grinned, "is going to think he's the centre of the universe."

Do we spoil this little guy? I wondered, looking down on the ball of ginger fluff perched on my slipper, head upside down, small body vibrating under a tiger-sized purr.

"Not spoiled, just enthusiastic," I thought I heard the Holy Spirit say. Knowing that "entheos" (Greek) means "inspired" I could see here, a parable in the making. With every inch of his being, Taffy responds to our loving care. We inspire that tiger-sized purr coming from that small, vibrating body. We are the centre of his universe, not the other way around.

"Taffy loves because we first loved him," I smiled as the scriptural declaration of 1 John 4:19, "We love because He first loved us," wound around in my head like joyful music. Here indeed was my parable. Just as Jesus used cultural artifacts of the day in His parables, I could see this kitten's loving response to our caring as a parable for our whole-hearted praise of our God.

Hallel is a form of scriptural praise, called "clamorously foolish". Hallel describes Taffy's state as he bounces his small energetic self into laps or onto slippers of his persons. When his persons sit together over an amiable cup of tea, he flies off for his fur toy, carrying it in his mouth into our midst like a small Irish terrier to wrestle it magnificently, watching from the corner of his eye for our approval. His reward for putting on such an enthusiastic display of appreciation is simply to be in our presence.

I've seen the posturing of our son's two adoring dogs as they fawn and frolic for their master's affection. Our kitten is not as commandingly handsome as those impressive fellows. But that day, I watched and was blessed as tiny Taffy sent his own love memo to our son the dog lover, curling up beside him on the sofa, looking into his face, blinking his button-sized eyes and stretching a tiny paw to the big hand beside him.

To be the loving friend of our Person is to find our reward just being in His presence. What other gift than the gift of love blesses both giver and receiver when given away...and blesses others in the giving as well?

I'm not a cat. My God is not some doting human entity. But the parable is seen in this similarity that the Lord takes pleasure in the joy we express when we come into His presence and abandon ourselves to exuberant hallel (1 Chronicles 23:30) praise.

Postscript: With Taffy on his leash, I took this parable to one of our church Sunday school classes. Seventy little pairs of eyes followed Taffy's jaunty stroll to the front of the classroom. I could guess the thoughts of the children: "What is a cat doing in church...and walking on a leash?"

Taffy sat on my shoulder while I told his five-minute story. On our way out, 70 children knew his "hallel" story and 70 pairs of little hands reached out to touch his fur as he passed down the aisle, fluffy tail held high, making friends at every step.

People who might be offended by someone "talking religion" will often relate easily and naturally to a tender story involving a child or a pet that tells of a real God genuinely moving to lavish a real blessing on a real life.

Nan McKenzie Kosowan

Biography

Nan McKenzie Kosowan

The writing bug bit me when my grade seven teacher had me read aloud to the class a story about a boy finding his lost puppy on Christmas Eve. When I sat down, there wasn't a dry eye in the room, including the teacher's and my own. I was impressed that a story from the heart could have such an effect on others. From that moment on, I looked forward with excitement to every writing assignment the teacher gave the class.

By the time I was in my final year of high school, my writing had been extended to a column for girls in The Canadian High News. My uncle, "Vernon Mac", an early editor of Macleans magazine, labeled my style "folksy" and told me to never change it.

After high school, I attended the University of Toronto and spent most of my time writing for the student newspaper, The Varsity. The editor set a course for my writing when he assigned to me a column profiling professorial staff. The profile is still my favorite genre of journalism. Bill, the assistant sports editor of The Varsity, liked to proofread my copy. (He still gives that oversight today.)

After graduation, I married Bill and started work as reporter, feature writer, columnist and woman's editor on a small town newspaper near Toronto. Once again, I saw how warmly everyday people can respond to stories that share life challenges, victories and joys.

Leaving that job to have our two kids, I missed writing about people and their passions. But life was full and rewarding for us when, as new Christians, we became part of the lay prayer and counseling team of our young church in Scarborough, Ontario. Those wonderful years passed quickly but other than producing an occasional magazine or newspaper article and our monthly church newsletter, I was doing little writing.

One day my wise, teenaged daughter heard me express a certain wistfulness to be writing again. "Mom," she said, "I see you being busy and happy, helping all sorts of people. And maybe you're a little sad because you don't really have time to do much writing now. But when you get back to your writing...and you will...what do you think you'll be writing about?"

Her thoughtful remarks came as an assurance from the Lord. Two decades later, I began to record stories gathered over many years of listening, sharing and praying with people. It wasn't until our daughter and son were finishing high school that I returned to my writing with a job on the staff of World Vision Canada. As a little side-adventure, I enjoyed writing and performing World Vision's radio spots. My son likes to tell about walking into his friend's room at Trinity Western College in British Columbia. As his friend reached to turn down his radio, Larry laughed and said, "Hey! Don't touch that dial, that's my mom!"

Lynda, that wise daughter, became a wise social worker, the executive director of a women's centre and our son became a correctional officer who writes on the side.

For the past 30 years, my cup, (or my inkwell?) has overflowed as I've freelanced for 11 Canadian denominational and interdenominational publications and three American magazines; *Charisma, Morningstar* and *SpiritLed Woman*. I have been a contributing author to *In Search of Hidden Heroes* by Don Moore and Lorna Dueck (Faith Today Publications, 1995), *My Turn To Care...Encouragement for Caregivers of Aging Parents* compiled and edited by Marlene Bagnull (Thomas Nelson Publishers, 1994 and Ampelos Press, 1999) and *God Answers Prayer* compiled and edited by Allison Bottke (Harvest House Publishers, 2005). In 2008, Guideposts Books series on *Miracles* used three of my stories: "God's Touch on a City Cat in the Wilds," "God Who?" and "How 'I-Forgive-You' Become Action Words."

For 18 years, I wrote a monthly column for the young, growing, regional church, Koinonia Christian Fellowship, in the Kitchener-Waterloo area of Ontario. The column, called "Caring", shared about God's help and wisdom available in our everyday lives. Serving on our church leadership team, my husband and I worked with people through whom God kept supplying me with real life stories of how He speaks into lives and orchestrates events to bless people...and make them a blessing! (Names used in this book are not always the actual names of the people in these true stories.)

What can touch someone's heart like a story of a changed life by a God who cares and wants to speak into our lives in so many different ways if we will choose to listen.

Nan McKenzie Kosowan

—ᏻᏩ—

CPSIA information can be obtained at www.ICGtesting.com
Printed in the USA
237553LV00004B/10/P

9 781896 213422